Sources and Strategies of Legal Research

Caroline L. Osborne

ASSOCIATE PROFESSOR OF LAW
DIRECTOR OF THE GEORGE R. FARMER JR. LAW LIBRARY
WEST VIRGINIA UNIVERSITY COLLEGE OF LAW

CAROLINA ACADEMIC PRESS
Durham, North Carolina

See catalog.loc.gov for complete
Library of Congress Cataloging-in-Publication Data

ISBN 978-1-5310-2623-3
eISBN 978-1-5310-2624-0

Carolina Academic Press
700 Kent Street
Durham, North Carolina 27701
(919) 489-7486
www.cap-press.com

Printed in the United States of America

Sources and Strategies of
Legal Research

This book is for my students—past, present, and future. It is informed by questions and confusion of the past with the hope my current and future students will benefit.

This work would not exist but for the help of friends and colleagues. Barbara, Carol, Jill, Joyce, Nick, Stephanie, there is no way I can appropriately reflect your contributions of time and support. I will simply say thank you!

CLO
April 2022

Contents

Part III | Search Strategies

Appendix

Attribution for Figures

Many thanks is extended to those who granted permission to use their content. Specifically, the material was reprinted with the permission of those indicated below.

Publisher	Figure(s)
Original content of author or as assignee or derivative work.	Figures 1.1, 1.2, 1.3, 1.4, 1.5, 1.6, 1.7, 1.8, 1.9, 1.10, 1.11, 1.12, 1.13, 1.14, 1.15, 1.16, 1.17, 2.1, 3.2, 3.3, 3.4, 4.1, 4.2, 4.3, 4.4, 4.5, 4.6, 4.7, 4.8. 4.9 4.10, 5.1, 5.2, 5.3, 5.4, 5.5, 5.6, 5.8, 6.1, 6.2, 6.3, 6.4, 6.5, 6.6, 6.7, 6.8, 7.2, 7.2, 7.4, 7.5, 7.6, 7.7, 7.8, 7.9, 8.2 , 10.1, 10.2, 11.1, 13.4, 14.1, 14.2, 14.3, 14.4, 16.1 20.1, 20.2, 20.3, 20.5, 20.6, 21.1, 22.6 and Appendices, A, B, C, D, E, F
West Academic Each such figure specified here is reprinted with the permission of West Academic.	Figures 13.1 and 13.2.
LexisNexis Each such figure specified here is reprinted from LexisNexis with permission. Copyright 2022 LexisNexis. All rights reserved.	Figures 1.18, 8.4, 8.5, 14.9, 14.10, 14.11, 16.2, 16.3, 16.4, 16.7, 16.8, 18.1, 18.2.
Thomson Reuters Each figure specified here is used and reprinted with the permission of Thomson Reuters.	Figures 5.6, 5.7, 8.1, 8.3, 9.1, 9.2, 9.3, 9.4, 9.5, 9.6, 11.2, 12.1, 13.3, 14.5, 14.6, 14.7, 14.8, 15.1, 15.2, 15.3, 16.5, 16.6, 17.1, 17.2, 17.3, 17.4, 18.3, 19.1, 19.2, 19.3, 19.4, 19.5, 19.6, 20.4, 22.1, 22.2.
Government Publishing Office	Figures 7.1, 7.3, 22.3, 22.4, 22.5, and Appendix G-1

List of Figures

Author's Note[1]

I know how to research and find information. Why do I need a class in legal research? I still recall thinking these thoughts in the fall semester of my first year of law school. Torts, property, civil procedure—this is where I needed to spend my time. That this thought has stayed with me for all of law school, practice, and now teaching indicates just how strongly I felt about legal research. If I knew then what I came to know in the next year of law school, I might have responded differently to my legal research class, perhaps with more diligence.

I was missing an important piece of information. I did not fully comprehend that finding the law, understanding the law, and analyzing the law as it applied to my question is the foundation of the practice of law. I'd researched many topics and written many papers as an undergraduate and I was successful in doing one kind of research. The incomplete part of my thought process, what I skipped over, was that I'd been taught how to do one kind of research, the tools, the sources, and the analysis. Now I needed to learn a different, specialized, type of research—legal research. I needed to learn where to find the law, what the different sources of law were, where to find materials explaining the, often, complex, state of the law and how to use that information to resolve my question.

I also missed another part of the puzzle. The simple questions, the ones that are settled law, are not the questions that require extensive research. As a law librarian at a large New York law firm ('big law') often tells their new associates—"If you can Google the answer your client

---

1. This book is made possible with the support of the West Virginia College of Law by the support and contribution of an Arthur B. Hodges Summer Research Grant to Caroline L. Osborne.

does not need you."[2] It is the novel question, the question that takes the law to a new place, the question that exists in the area where there is no clear statement of the law, these are the questions that lawyers spend time litigating and arguing. In contrast, law school assignments are neatly packaged to focus on the material being taught—rules, cases, statutes. Practice is messy. Legal questions are not neatly packaged. It is rarely as easy as the law school assignment seems. Your supervising attorney will not be impressed if you spend hours figuring out how to research rather than reading, analyzing, and analogizing the law. Finding cases, statutes, regulations, and constitutional provisions is merely the first step in a research quest. The other step is analyzing what you've found for relevance to answer your question. Legal analysis, understanding and applying the law, crafting an analogy out of the law that is there, is the missing piece of research. The foundation of legal research is finding, understanding, analyzing, and applying the law.

Finding law in an era of information excess, information overload, is easy. Finding authentic and reliable information that is relevant and addresses the legal problem before your client, is difficult. It might even be argued, successfully, that the vast amount of information at our fingertips makes effective and efficient research more difficult. Consider that this bounty of information makes the need for excellent research skills and efficient and effective research and analysis a critical skill of a successful lawyer.

This text is unique from other legal research texts. The materials are divided into three parts. Part I focuses on the mechanics or basics of law such as the court system, legal authority, precedent, research strategy or planning, legal analysis, and legal citation. Part II focuses on the sources of law including both those that contain the law, the tools that assist one in locating the law, and sources that comment and explain. Part III addresses search strategies—strategies that the researcher employs to effectively and efficiently locate materials to assist in answering the legal question.

CAROLINE OSBORNE
January 2022

---

2. Anonymous quote from NY Law Librarian at Big Law firm made at AALS Annual Meeting (January 2014).

Part I

The Mechanics of Legal Research

Chapter 1

Authority and the Court System

The objective of any research assignment is to advise your client with accurate solutions to their legal problems. To do that successfully, you must know and understand the law as it applies in that specific instance. The words *specific instance* are important. Each problem is unique in some way, especially for the client. Understanding the nuance and novelty of your client's question and the application of the law considering such nuance and novelty is fundamental. The starting point for research is a deep understanding of the legal system and resulting sources of law.

LEARNING OBJECTIVES

- Analyze legal information for application to a legal issue.
- Distinguish among the types of legal authority recognizing when and where they should be used.
- Understand the hierarchy of legal precedent.
- Analyze legal information for fit to apply to a legal issue.
- Formulate a preliminary issue statement for any research problem.

The Legal System

Our legal system is a dual system in parallel at the federal and state levels. This dual legal system is comprised of three coequal branches of government: the judiciary, executive, and legislative branches exists at the federal, territories, and each of the fifty states. Consider the coequal branches of government as the maker, the enforcer, and the interpreter. The executive branch enforces the statutes created by the legislature. The legislative branch makes law in the form of statutes, and the judiciary interprets the statutes made by the legislature. The executive and judicial branches have derivative powers to support the law-making function of the legislature through implementational and interpretative functions, which result in legal authority.

Completing the universe of laws are those that exist at the local level—local government or municipal law. These laws address topics of daily life. Laws at the local level involve zoning or land use, business, education, and property taxes, as examples of common subjects. Municipal law tends to be specific to a city or county and the associated governmental bodies within such city or county.

Legal Authority Defined

Legal authority—a source of law stating a legal rule, legal doctrine, or legal reasoning that may be used as a basis for a decision or argument.

There are four key sources of law existing at the federal and state levels. They are constitutions, statutes (passed by the legislature), judicial opinions (handed down by the judiciary), and rules or regulations from the administrative state (promulgated by the executive). Three other sources of law are created by the executive branch and include executive orders, proclamations, and administrative decisions.[1] The phrase *law-making capacity* is key in the determination of what is law. It is only the product created in the law-making capacity that is the law. Justices Scalia and Ginsburg, speaking by invitation at George Mason Law School, while interesting, do not act in their *law-making capacity* and create no law in their remarks. In contrast, a United States Supreme

---

1. An executive order is the signed, written directive of the President, a product of the executive branch and requires no approval from Congress. They have the force of law, are initially published in the Federal Register, and later codified in Title 3 of the C.F.R. Congressional legislation may overturn an executive order or action by a sitting President. Proclamations are similar but focus on information relating to holidays, commemoration, and trade. Administrative decisions are quasi-judicial in nature made by administrative law judges with reasoned analysis, findings of fact and conclusions of law. They are non-binding in the absence of substantial evidence and subject to judicial review on questions of law. Administrative decisions are governed by the Administrative Procedure Act. American Bar Association, *What is an Executive Order?*, available at https://www.american bar.org/groups/public_education/publications/teaching-legal-docs/what-is-an-executive -order-/ (last visited May 13, 2022).

Court majority decision authored by Scalia is law as it is created in the law-making capacity of the judicial branch. As an initial step in your analysis of a source, you should always ask if the source is a product of the law-making authority of the branch of government.

We have fifty-one constitutions: the federal constitution, and a constitution from each state. In addition to these fifty-one constitutions, our territories also have constitutions. A constitution may be written or unwritten. An unwritten constitution is more precisely referred to as an uncodified constitution.[2] The constitution creates the framework of government. The frame defines the boundaries of the government's authority as granted to the government by the people. The federal constitution is the foremost source of law. All laws, whether federal or state, must be in accord with the precepts of the federal constitution.

In our dual legal system, each state has its own government that acts in parallel to the federal system. Just like the federal government has a constitution, legislature, executive, and judiciary, each state has a constitution, legislature, executive, and judiciary. A state through its constitution creates its own frame that sets different boundaries from that of the federal constitution. A state may elect to grant rights that exceed those granted by the federal constitution. However, a state constitution cannot grant fewer rights than those granted under the federal constitution as the state constitution is subordinate to the federal constitution. The duality of the legal system also requires that any law created by a state must comply with both the federal constitution and its state constitution.

The topics of federal and state law are generally distinct. Topics governed by federal law traditionally include interstate commerce, immigration, bankruptcy, civil rights law, coins, copyright and patents, and federal criminal laws like counterfeiting. By comparison, state law topics tend to focus on matters of private concern such as contracts, criminal

---

2. Canada, New Zealand, China, Israel, and the United Kingdom are examples of countries with uncodified constitutions. An uncodified constitution is one in which fundamental rules are derived from custom, precedent, statutes, and other legal instruments. The constitution is understood through judicial commentary and expert commentary. *Countries with Uncodified Constitutions,* available at https://www.worldatlas.com/articles /countries-with-uncodified-constitutions.html (last visited May 13, 2022).

law, torts, property, family law, and workers' compensation. A further division is that of local government or municipal law with topics focusing on zoning, traffic, construction, and local health and safety. Some topics overlap and others have a dual presence. For example, tax may involve a federal, state, or local law depending upon the question. Some topics like criminal law and marriage have overlapping presences in federal and state law. Criminal laws governing marijuana are one example. Some states have legalized medical marijuana, but cannabis remains a controlled substance under federal law.[3]

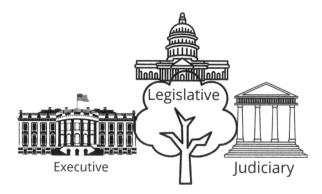

Figure 1.1 Three Coequal Branches of Government

The structure of the three coequal branches of our government reflects the duality of the system. Each branch has a specific role.

- The legislative branch, the maker, creates law in the form of statutes. As part of the checks and balances of the law-making process resulting in the statute, executive branch action is the final step in creating a law.
- The executive branch, the enforcer, is tasked with enforcing the laws created by the legislature. In addition, the executive possesses its own law-making authority. Administrative agencies fall under the umbrella of the executive branch. The Federal Bureau of Investigation (FBI), the Environmental Protection Agency

---

3. 21 U.S.C. §812 (2022).

(EPA), and the Department of Commerce are examples of federal administrative agencies. At the state level, the State Bureau of Investigation (SBI) and the Division of Motor Vehicles (DMV) are examples of state administrative agencies. We often refer to the agencies as the *administrative state*. The executive branch through its agencies enforces the laws created by the legislature. The executive branch also possesses a derivative law-making authority via a specific delegation of authority from the legislature to the executive by which the executive branch is empowered to create law in the form of a rule to facilitate the charge of the legislature as embodied in the statute. This power is derivative and circumscribed by the specific grant of authority. These rules, also called regulations, fill in gaps in the statutory language and implementation and provide the detail that is often needed to complete the intent of the legislation.

- The judiciary is the interpreter. They write judicial opinions that interpret the language of statutes and regulations promulgated by the legislative and executive branches, respectively. The judiciary has the authority to determine that a statute or rule fails to meet the requirements of a constitution abrogating the statute or the rule as unconstitutional. Courts also apply statutes and rules to the matter before it to resolve the conflict before the court. Courts also have the authority to create their own law. Laws created by the court are called *common law,* As a court may invalidate a statute finding it unconstitutional, a legislature may negate the common law created by judicial opinion by passing a new legislative act.

Among statutes, regulations, and judicial opinions, all sources of primary authority, these are distinct. Regulations are derivative and confined by the enabling statute authorizing the creation of regulations on the specific topic. Judicial opinions apply the common law to a set of facts, creating an interpretation in that specific instance or apply a statute or a regulation to a set of facts, creating an interpretation of the application of the statute or regulation to that specific instance. A constitutional provision is the most permanent and supreme law and is interpreted by the judiciary.

What happens when primary authorities challenge one another? The answer depends upon the type of primary authority. Below are examples that illustrate common types of challenges.

Examples

The Georgia state constitution includes a provision restricting the right to vote to white male property owners. This state constitutional provision will fail scrutiny under the equal protection and other clauses of the federal constitution. The federal constitution prevails.

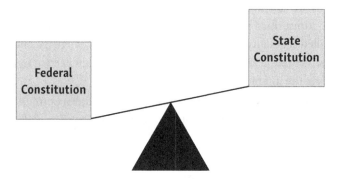

Figure 1.2 Example of Federal v. State Constitution—Primary Authority

A federal statute prohibits the practice of the religion of Buddhism. The federal statute will fail under the First Amendment freedom of religion provisions. The federal constitution prevails.

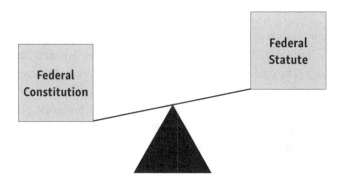

Figure 1.3 Federal Constitution v. Federal Statute—Primary Authority

Virginia state statute requirements for marriage displace the common law marriage provision that cohabitation for seven years created a marriage by default. The state statute prevails over prior common law.

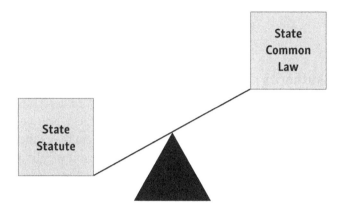

Figure 1.4 State Statute v. State Common Law—Primary Authority

In a matter contesting a rule that protects migratory birds promulgated under the Clean Water Act (federal), the rule will fail if the court interprets the rule as exceeding the authority delegated to the Environmental Protection Agency under the enabling statute of the Clean Water Act. The federal regulation fails as it exceeded the derivative authority as delegated by the legislature to the executive branch.

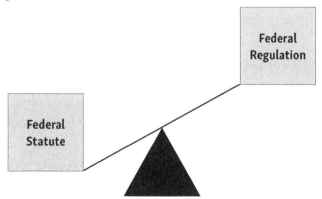

Figure 1.5 Federal Statute v. Federal Regulation—Primary Authority

Branch of Government and Law and Type of Law		
Legislature	*Executive*	*Judicial*
Statutes	Rules or regulations	Judicial opinions
	Executive orders and Promulgations	

Figure 1.6 Branch of Government and Law and Type of Law

Legal Authority

Legal authority is a comprehensive term used to describe types of legal information. It is critical to remember that legal sources are not created equally. Some have more influence or weight than others. Often circumstance will dictate the level of importance and weight of the authority. In law we customarily divide legal sources into two broad categories—primary authority and secondary authority. Primary authority is the law, using the term *law* in its broad and general meaning. Statutes, rules, regulations, constitutional provisions, and judicial opinions are all types of primary authority because they are law. Anything that is not the law falls into the category of secondary authority. These are materials or sources that explain or comment on the law or tools that assist in locating the law. It is imperative to classify a source as either primary or secondary, as an argument made to the court must be based on primary authority. Secondary authority may be used to find the law or buttress or flesh out an argument. An argument cannot exclusively be based on secondary authority. Put another way, secondary authority never controls the outcome as all secondary authorities are nonbinding.

The Stakes

Why is understanding authority so important? What happens if you submit a brief to a court that relies exclusively on persuasive authority and omits the primary, binding authority?

Your client loses as a legal argument must be premised on primary binding authority.

The authority decision tree is one method of quickly determining the authority of a source. Answering the questions at each step of the decision tree permits you to classify any source of authority easily and correctly.

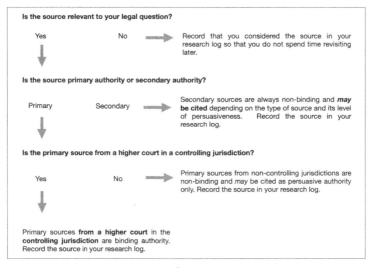

Figure 1.7 Authority Decision Tree

Step 1: Relevance

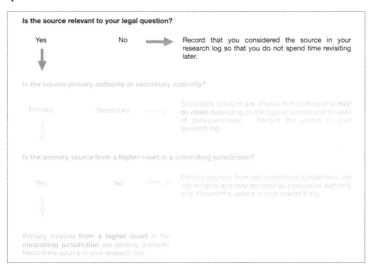

Figure 1.8 Authority Decision Tree — Step 1: Relevance Highlighted

Relevance is the initial step in your analysis. Step 1 asks you to determine if the source is relevant. Think of relevance as *fit*. How does the source add to your understanding or knowledge of the legal question? Does the source act as a relevant precedent? Does it speak directly to your question? Does it explain or comment on your matter? Does it advance your research by suggesting other resources, search terms, or other items of value? How might you use the information in the source to move forward with your research? If the source in any way adds benefit to your research process, the source is relevant. If you determine the source has no relevance, you document that you considered the source, determined it was not relevant, and move on to your next source.

Relevance

Many struggle with the concept of relevance. Think about *relevance* in your everyday life. You visit your doctor to discuss your exercise regimen. You share your Spotify playlist, that you play tennis twice a week, attend Pilates twice a week, and have a Peloton bike you ride each evening What is the information your doctor needs to know to answer your questions about the benefits of your exercise regimen? Your existing exercise routine is relevant but what about your Spotify playlist? In this instance, the Spotify playlist is **not relevant**.

Step 2: Type of Authority—Primary v. Secondary Authority

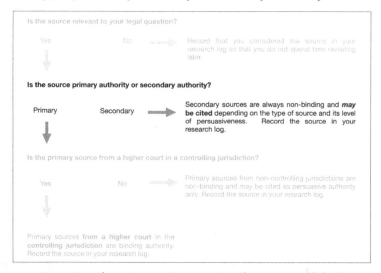

Figure 1.9 Authority Decision Tree—Step 2: Authority Type Highlighted

Once you determine a source is relevant to your research, your next or second step is to classify the source as primary or secondary. If the source is a constitution, statute, judicial opinion, or regulation, the source is law and is classified as primary authority. If the source is none of these, the source is *not law* and is classified as secondary authority.

Step 3: Weight of Authority—Binding v. Non-Binding, Persuasive

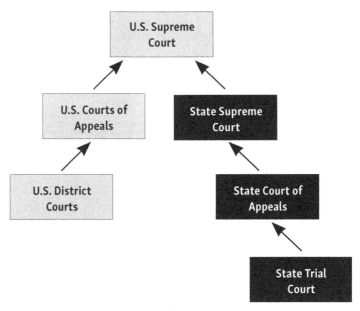

Figure 1.10 The Dual Court System

Weight of authority is how we discuss the power the authority asserts on the answer to a legal question. Authorities vary in degree of weight with the first question being if the source is primary or secondary and the second question being if the source is binding or nonbinding.

Weight Defined

Weight—(1) degree of persuasive influence; (2) ability or power to influence a decision

This final step, the third step of your analysis, asks if the authority is binding (the terms *binding* and *mandatory authority* are used interchangeably) or nonbinding (the terms *nonbinding* and *persuasive* are used interchangeably). Binding or mandatory authority is authority a court is required to follow. Nonbinding or persuasive authority is authority a court may elect to be persuaded by but is not required to consider.

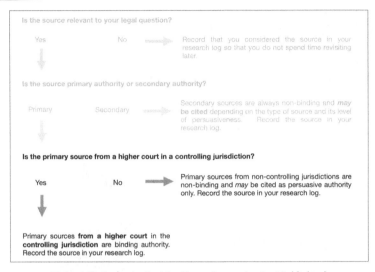

Figure 1.11 Authority Decision Tree—Determination Highlighted

Once you classify a source as primary, you must then consider the question of jurisdiction. Jurisdiction, here, is not jurisdiction in the sense of civil procedure—where will I file my lawsuit, or venue. Here, jurisdiction is best thought of as the controlling jurisdiction. What court has the authority to speak to my question? Put another way, controlling jurisdiction is the jurisdiction that issues binding authority for your legal question. A judicial opinion is primary, binding authority only when the issuing jurisdiction is the controlling jurisdiction. If the opinion is issued from outside the controlling jurisdiction, the decision becomes primary, persuasive authority.

The classification of binding or nonbinding is based on whether the primary authority is issued by the controlling jurisdiction. Determining if a source is binding or nonbinding is more complicated than the categorization of primary or secondary. If you classify a source as secondary authority you also classify the source as nonbinding, as a secondary source may never be binding authority. The complication is found in classifying primary authorities. Primary authorities may be classified as

binding or nonbinding. Jurisdiction and court hierarchy are the determining factors of binding or nonbinding status and, accordingly, weight.
This a binary determination. Primary sources are either binding or nonbinding.

Step 3: Determining Weight of Primary Authority

1. Identify the controlling jurisdiction and compare to the issuing court.
2. Is the issuing court a higher court within the controlling
   jurisdiction?

Importance of the Court Hierarchy

Controlling jurisdiction is only one factor in the determination of
binding or nonbinding. If you determine the opinion is issued by the
controlling jurisdiction, you must also determine which court issued
the opinion and the position of such court within the hierarchy of the
court system.

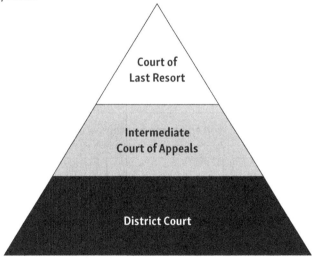

Figure 1.12 Court Hierarchy

The federal system consists of three levels of courts. At the bottom are
the United States District Courts as the trial courts. Each state has at
least one federal trial or district court. The United States Courts of Ap-

peals are the intermediate courts of appeals that hear appeals from the trial courts. The United States Court of Appeals is divided into thirteen circuits comprised of the Federal Circuit, the District of Columbia, and Circuits numbered 1 to 11 based on geographical boundaries across the United States.

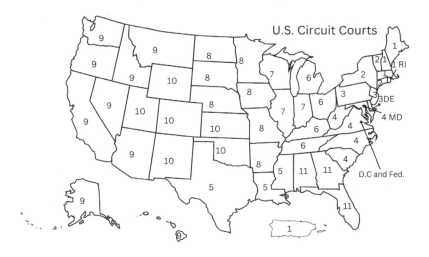

Figure 1.13 United States Court of Appeals Circuits

The court of last resort for the federal system is the United States Supreme Court.

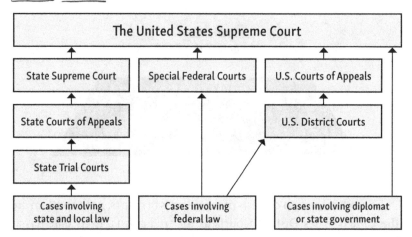

Figure 1.14 State and Federal Court Hierarchy in Parallel

Trial courts bind the parties to the case and no other. As a rule of thumb when considering the authority of a court, courts bind down — not across or up. As the trial courts bind only the constituent parties, their decisions are classified as primary, persuasive, or primary, non-binding authority even within the controlling jurisdiction.

The trial court is at the bottom of the hierarchy with no court below to bind. The decisions of the intermediate courts of appeals bind the trial courts below them, binding down. In the federal system and some state systems, there are multiple courts of appeals. As courts bind down (vertically) and not across (horizontally), the decisions of an intermediate court of appeal would be primary, persuasive in a neighboring court or a court at an equivalent point in the court hierarchy. For example, the decisions of the Fourth Circuit are primary, binding authority to the federal district courts (trial courts) of the Fourth Circuit but primary, persuasive authority to the Fifth Circuit and the United States Supreme Court. When circuits reach different outcomes or interpretations on the same legal issue, we refer to this as a circuit court split. Thus, the law may differ depending upon the circuit. This difference remains unless and until the Supreme Court resolves the difference by handing down a decision of its own, binding the circuit courts and resolving the split.

The decisions of the court of last resort are primary, binding authority to the trial courts and the intermediate courts of appeals within its jurisdiction. Remember, courts bind down. For example, the decisions of the North Carolina Supreme Court are primary, binding authority to the North Carolina Courts of Appeals and the North Carolina trial courts but primary, persuasive authority to a Virginia or South Carolina court. The U.S. Supreme Court possesses nationwide jurisdiction with the power to decide appeals involving issues of federal law originating in either federal or state court.

In some states, the intermediate court of appeals does not exist, resulting in an appeal from the trial court to the court of last resort. The court of last resort is commonly called the supreme court although nomenclature is not uniformly applied. For example, in New York State the trial court is called the supreme court.

The dual court system depicted in Figure 1.15 represents two separate court systems meeting solely at the U.S. Supreme Court, the court of

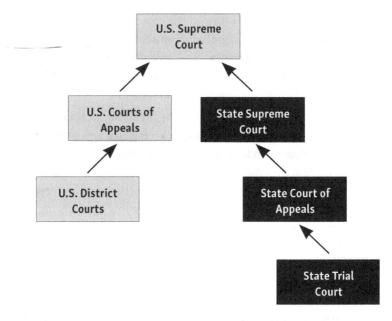

Figure 1.15 The Dual Court System (Repeated)

last resort. Opinions from the federal court system are from the federal jurisdiction do not bind courts in the state court systems except for opinions issued from the U.S. Supreme Court. Remember, courts bind down—not across—and primary, binding authority requires the decision to be from the same jurisdiction.

Returning to the question of weight of authority, is the opinion issued by higher court within the controlling jurisdiction? If the answer is yes, the opinion is from your controlling jurisdiction and a higher court, then the opinion is binding, primary authority. If the answer is no, the opinion is either not from the controlling jurisdiction or the opinion is not from a higher court, then the opinion is primary, persuasive authority.

What about a state statute, regulation, or constitutional provision from outside the controlling jurisdiction? While they remain primary authority and are binding, primary authority within their own jurisdictions, such state statutes, regulations, and constitutional provisions do not apply outside their own jurisdiction. Said another way, the state constitutional, statutory, and regulatory provisions—while law and primary authority—are neither persuasive nor binding outside their original jurisdiction. They lack any weight beyond the controlling jurisdiction.

Once you determine the type of authority, you must assess the persuasive value the authority brings to your argument. Consider again the decision tree. In Step 1 you considered the relevance of the source to your question. You asked how the source adds to your knowledge or understanding. A source that is relevant, that adds to your knowledge has some degree of weight. The question is how much? How persuasive is the source?

In Step 2 of the decision tree, you classified the authority as primary or secondary. Secondary sources may assist you in understanding and finding the law. Some secondary sources may be cited to support your argument. Factors such as type of secondary source will bear on the persuasive value of your source. Consider the persuasive value of secondary sources as existing on a continuum with no persuasive value for certain sources and a high degree of persuasive value for other sources. Expertise and reputation of the author and publisher, currency of material, depth of discussion, and similarity of legal issue and facts are all factors in considering the degree of persuasion. The persuasive value of different sources is discussed in detail in Part II.

Figure 1.16 Persuasive Value Continuum

In Step 3 of the decision tree, you classified the authority as binding or nonbinding. Secondary sources are always nonbinding. By contrast, a source that is classified as secondary, persuasive, not authored by an expert, and is cursory in depth of treatment exists at the opposite end of the continuum with little persuasive value.

Examples of Persuasive Value and Source Type		
Source	*Authority*	*Value*
Case from highest court in controlling jurisdiction with same or similar facts and the same legal issue.	Primary, binding authority as the authority is law from the highest court in your controlling jurisdiction	Highest value due to stare decisis. Court must follow.
State legal encyclopedia article speaking directly to your legal issue	Secondary, non-binding authority.	Low value. This source has minimal depth of discussion and is not authored by an expert. It is also secondary. To be used in the research process only. See Chapter 8 for additional detail on legal encyclopedia.
Statute from controlling jurisdiction	Primary, binding authority	Highest value. Court must follow.
Statute from outside the controlling jurisdiction	Primary, persuasive authority	None
Case from trial court in controlling jurisdiction	Primary, persuasive authority	Low value. Trial courts bind the parties, not the court. If this is the initial instance of the legal issue being addressed, the decision of the trial court will have some minimal persuasive value.

Figure 1.17 Persuasive Value and Source Type Examples

Example

I am in a Target store in Charlotte, North Carolina, when I slip and fall due to someone who left a leaky bottle of baby oil on the floor. The manager of the store was informed of the presence of the spill where it remained for several hours before I slipped and fell due to the oil resulting in injury.

This is an example of the classic tort of negligence. The accident happened in North Carolina; I will bring suit in a state trial court in North Carolina (the venue). This is a question of state tort law and specifically North Carolina state tort law. Thus, the controlling jurisdiction is the state of North Carolina. As the controlling jurisdiction, North Carolina state law will constitute binding primary authority to determine the outcome of my slip-and-fall lawsuit.

How does this example fit into the dual court systems in the United States? There are fifty-one separate jurisdictions. The federal system is its own jurisdiction, and each state is its own jurisdiction. As the question is one of state law,[4] that state's court will decide the outcome. If the question is one of federal law, the federal courts would determine the outcome. What about the tort law of Virginia, or South Carolina, or federal law? In the slip-and-fall example above, federal law or the state laws of Virginia and South Carolina are still primary authority. Virginia, South Carolina, and federal each constitute a separate jurisdiction. Cases from the federal system and the neighboring states of Virginia and South Carolina are still the law and, as such, primary authority. However, cases from these jurisdictions are not from my controlling jurisdiction and therefore are primary, nonbinding or primary, persuasive authority. What about a statute, regulation, or constitutional provision from Virginia or South Carolina? While they remain primary authority and are binding, primary authority within their own states, the statutes, regulations, and constitutional provisions do not apply outside their own jurisdiction. Said another way, the constitutional, statutory, and regulatory provisions—while law and primary authority—are neither persuasive nor binding outside their original jurisdiction. They lack any weight beyond the controlling jurisdiction.

Sometimes a court must consider the law outside its own jurisdiction to reach a decision in the matter before it. For example, the Federal Dis-

---

4. A general rule of thumb is to think about your 1L courses when determining if a question is one of federal or state law. Property, torts, contracts, and criminal law tend to be state law questions. Constitutional law questions tend to be federal. Procedural questions can be either state or federal depending upon the situs of the suit.

trict Court in the Eastern District of North Carolina hears a case that includes a tort claim. Torts are traditionally governed by state law rather than federal law. In this instance the Federal District Court would apply North Carolina state tort law to determine the outcome. More specifically, the federal judge will look to the decisions of the North Carolina Supreme Court and North Carolina Courts of Appeals as primary, binding authority to determine the outcome of the tort issue. What authority is the resulting opinion of a federal district court in an unrelated North Carolina tort matter? As the federal courts are a separate jurisdiction, the decision from the federal trial court to a North Carolina court is primary, persuasive. Remember your decision tree. The decision is the product of the law-making capacity of the judiciary and as such a law. As a law the source is classified as primary authority. Next, we note the decision is outside the controlling jurisdiction and a decision of the trial court indicating that the decision is nonbinding or persuasive. Our conclusion is that the opinion of the North Carolina federal district court on North Carolina tort law is primary, persuasive authority.

Your objective in researching is to locate sufficient information to make a sound legal argument. To do so, you require information that is (1) relevant, (2) primary, binding authority, and (3) secondary authority that assists you in understanding the authority. Your research is complete when you find all primary, binding authority that addresses your question, including authority that is not favorable to your argument. In addition, you may also wish to find primary, persuasive authorities that will buttress your argument and help persuade the court to your position. Use of primary, persuasive authority is especially useful when addressing a matter of first impression to the jurisdiction. Excellent researchers understand when to spend time researching for primary, persuasive authority and when to not.

First Impression Defined

We refer to an issue as one of first impression when there is no primary authority addressing the matter in the controlling jurisdiction. It is the first time this issue has come to the controlling jurisdiction.

Why do I need to find all the primary, binding authority? Is it insufficient to simply locate the primary, binding authority that supports my argument, my client's position? The answer is yes, it is insufficient. You are required to find everything, both the authority that favors your position and the authority that is not favorable to your client. There are multiple reasons. The first reason is ethical. You are required to acknowledge unfavorable authority to the court. That reason is sufficient in and of itself, but there are other reasons. You need to understand contra authority to evaluate the success of your client's position and advise your client accordingly. You will also need to be prepared to respond to the unfavorable authority on behalf of your client.

Precedent and Stare Decisis

Precedent is a foundation of our law. The principle of precedent states that a rule of law created by the judiciary becomes authority for future, similar instances and decisions. Our system is based on common law, which is predicated on the principle of stability. Common law is grounded in the belief that there is an unwritten way, a custom, of doing things, common to society.[5] When we abide by that custom, we create predictable outcomes that promote stability and reliance. In the early development of the common law judges did not make law, so much as reduce the custom to law, memorializing the custom in writing, thus documenting the custom as the *common law*. At that point, once the custom was written down it became the established legal principle preserved as of the time of the writing. Once written, the legal principle is settled law and is available for others to reference and rely upon in similar circumstances. The process of the use of precedent became the doctrine of stare decisis. So ingrained is the concept of precedent in the original thirteen colonies that the colonies, and now the states, adopted the *common law of England* by statute.[6]

---

5. Our system, excluding Louisiana, is founded on English common law. Louisiana's legal system is predicated on civil law. The civil law system is based on the Roman legal system principally located in Europe and Latin America. Common law systems emphasize judicial opinions, custom and stare decisis while civil law systems emphasize laws made by the legislature.

6. VA. CODE ANN. §1-200 (2022).

§ 1-200. The common law.

The common law of England, insofar as it is not repugnant to the principles of the Bill of Rights and Constitution of this Commonwealth, shall continue in full force within the same, and be the rule of decision, except as altered by the General Assembly.

Figure 1.18 Va. Code Ann. §1-200 (Virginia Statutory Provision Adopting English Common Law)

Applies HORIZONTALLY and VERTICALLY same JURISDICTION

Stare decisis is Latin, meaning "let the decision stand." The doctrine of stare decisis creates an obligation on the court to rely on existing precedent in reaching their decision. The goal of stare decisis is to create stability and predictability in the law.

> *Stare decisis* plays an important role in our case law, and we have explained that it serves many valuable ends. It protects the interests of those who have taken action in reliance on a past decision. It "reduces incentives for challenging settled precedents, saving parties and courts the expense of endless relitigation. It fosters "evenhanded" decisionmaking by requiring that like cases be decided in a like manner. It "contributes to the actual and perceived integrity of the judicial process." And it restrains judicial hubris and reminds us to respect the judgement of those who have grappled with the important questions in the past. "Precedent is a way of accumulating and passing down the learning of past generations."[7]

The establishment of our legal system on the concept of precedent and the doctrine of stare decisis dictates that a researcher locates the primary, binding authority on the topic. A good researcher will find the universe of existing cases that constitute precedent. "*Like determines like*" meaning cases with the same or similar factual predicate and the same or similar legal issue should have the similar outcomes. Thus, precedent is the use of prior legal decisions as a basis for deciding new controversaries. Intermediate courts of appeals and courts of last

---

7. Dobbs v. Jackson Women's Health Organization, 142 S.Ct. 2228 (2022) (internal reference omitted).

resort are usually hesitant to deviate from their prior rulings absent a
compelling argument. However, in the face of a compelling argument,
they may elect change and are not bound by their prior opinions. Policy
arguments, change in circumstances, unforeseen application, and general evolution of the law, may all present compelling circumstances for
a court to elect change.[8]

There is considerable debate among the justices at the Supreme Court
as to the standard that should apply when considering overturning existing precedent. In the 1992 decision of *Planned Parenthood v. Casey*
the court suggests that the decision to overrule prior precedent is informed by a series of *"prudential and pragmatic considerations designed
to test the consistency of overruling a prior decision with the ideal of the
rule of law and to gauge the respective costs of reaffirming and overruling
a case."*[9] In *Casey*, three justices suggested a four-part test for overruling
existing precedent.

1. Workability—Has the rule/precedent proven to be "intolerable
   in defying practical workability?"[10]
2. Reliance interests—The presence reliance interests the recis-
   sion of which would create hardship or inequity.[11]
3. Presence of changes in the law to make the precedent outdated
   statement of abandoned doctrine.[12]
4. A significant change in facts to render little or no practical application of the precedent.[13]

Citizens United v. Federal Election Commission[14] and *Janus v. American Federation of State, County and Municipal Employees, Council 31*[15]

---

8. *See generally* Margaret N. Kniffen, *Overruling Supreme Court Precedent: Anticipa-
tory Actions by the United States Courts of Appeals,* 51 FORDHAM L. REV. 52 (2012); Joseph
W. Mead, *Stare Decisis in the Inferior Courts of the United States*, 12 NEV. L. REV. 787 (2012).
   9. Planned Parenthood v. Casey, 505 U.S. 833, 854 (1992).
   10. *Id.*
   11. *Id.*
   12. *Id.*
   13. *Id.*
   14. Citizens United v. Federal Election Comm'n, 558 U.S. 310 (2010).
   15. Janus v. American Fed., 138 S. Ct. 2448 (2018).

provided further guidance as to when a court of last resort might over-rule its own prior decision. *Citizens United* sets out a four-factor test for deciding if adherence to *stare decisis* is proper. The factors are:

1. Workability
2. Age of decision
3. Presence of reliance interests[16]
4. Is the decision well-reasoned or quality of the precedent's reasoning.[17]

These Supreme Court decisions suggest deviation from existing precedent is rare and *"our precedent is to be respected unless the most convincing of reasons demonstrates that adherence to it puts us on a course that is sure error."*[18] However, "in appropriate circumstances we must be willing to reconsider, and if necessary, overrule constitutional decisions."[19] The recognition of the value of precedent is similarly noted in the *Janus* court's language of *"stare decisis is the preferred course because it promotes the evenhanded, predictable, and consistent development of legal principles, fosters reliance on judicial decisions and contributes to the actual and perceived integrity of the judicial process."*[20] In *Citizens United*, the Supreme Court noted that consideration also should be given to *"whether experience has pointed up the precedent's shortcomings"* concluding that *"[w]hen neither party defends the reasoning of a precedent, the principle of adhering to that precedent through stare decisis is diminished."*[21] This is similar to the fifth factor of the test articulated in *Janus* requiring evaluation of *"consistence with related decisions."*[22]

---

16. A reliance interest is defined in Citizens United as "important considerations in property and contract cases where parties may have acted in conformance with existing legal rules in order to conduct transactions." *Id.* at 365.
17. *Id.* at 363.
18. *Id.*
19. *Dobbs* at 2262.
20. *Janus* at 2478 (*quoting* Payne v. Tennessee, 501 U.S. 808, 827 (1991)).
21. *Citizens United* at 363.
22. *Janus* at 2478–79.

"Super precedents are those constitutional decisions in which public institutions have heavily invested, repeatedly relied, and consistently supported over a significant period. Super precedents are deeply embedded into our law and lives through the subsequent activities of the other branches. Super precedents seep into the public consciousness and become a fixture of the legal framework."[23]

Are there precedents that are so fundamental that they are quasi constitutional and exist beyond the scope of overruling, so called *super precedents*? Some legal scholars espouse the theory of the *super precedent*.[24] Originally suggested by Judge Michael Luttig,[25] the idea of a super precedent in constitutional law suggests a decision involving constitutional law doctrine where the correctness of the decision is so settled that it is not a matter in which a court will expend its limited resources.[26] In short, the rule of law for which the precedent stands is long settled and promotes the values of stare decisis—consistency, stability, predictability, and reliance.[27] Legal theorists suggest that classification as a super precedent confers the status of a landmark opinion in constitutional law and, accordingly, such super precedents are immune from threat of reversal.[28] Suggested examples of cases qualifying as super precedent include: *Marbury v. Madison*[29] (judicial review), *Mapp v. Ohio*[30] (unreasonable search and seizure/4th Amendment), *Luther v. Borden*[31] (political question doctrine), and *Brown v. Board of Education*[32] (mandating school desegregation/striking down separate but equal).[33] Gerhardt notes that infamy does not confer super precedent

23. Michael J. Gerhardt, *Super Precedent*, 90 MINN. L. REV. 1204, 05 (2006).
24. *See generally* Michael J. Gerhardt, *Super Precedent*, 90 MINN. L. REV. 1204 (2006).
25. Richmond Med. Ctr. For Women v. Gilmore, 219 F.3d 376, 376–77 (4th Cir. 2000).
26. Michel J. Gerhardt, *Super Precedent* at 1204.
27. *Id*. at 1206.
28. *Id*.
29. Marbury v. Madison, 5 U.S. (1 Cranch) 137 (1803).
30. Mapp v. Ohio, 367 U.S. 643 (1961).
31. Luther v. Borden, 48 U.S. (7 How.) 1 (1849).
32. Brown v. Board of Education, 347 U.S. 483 (1954).
33. *See* Michel J. Gerhardt, *Super Precedent*.

status and notoriety must be distinguished from accepted law.[34] Super precedents may be difficult to identify but they share the common descriptive features of:

1. Establishes basic framework or propositions of constitutional law.
2. Consistent reinforcement at the national level from Congress, the Court, and society.
3. Provides foundation for further development of constitutional doctrine in one or more areas.[35]

In *Dobbs v. Jackson Women's Health Organization*, the Supreme Court delineated the current factors for consideration in determining if a court should depart from current precedent. The five factors are:[36]

1. Determination of and nature of error,[37]
2. Quality of reasoning (presence or absence of grounding in the text, history, or precedent of the constitution and justification for limits versus arbitrary line drawing),[38]
3. Workability of the rules imposed (may the rule established be "understood and applied in a consistent and predicable manner").[39]
4. Disruptive effect on other areas of law, (distortion of unrelated legal doctrine), and [40]
5. Absence of concrete reliance.[41]

In sum, the majority in *Dobbs* indicated that precedent is to be respected but not act as a straitjacket.[42]

---

34. *Id.*
35. *Id.*
36. *Dobbs* at 2265–2280.
37. *Id.* at 2265.
38. *Id.* at 2266.
39. *Id.* at 2272.
40. *Id.* at 2275.
41. *Id.* at 2276.
42. *Id.* at 2280.

To illustrate, the role of precedent, consider again our slip-and-fall example.

Example

I am in a Target store in Charlotte, North Carolina when I slip and fall due to someone who left a leaky bottle of baby oil on the floor. The manager of the store was informed of the presence of the spill where it remained for several hours before I slipped and fell due to the oil resulting in injury.

Your legal question is whether Target is responsible for the injuries received due to their negligence in leaving the leaky bottle of baby oil in the aisle creating a dangerous environment for the customer that resulted in a customer's fall. In your research you located two cases. Case A is from the North Carolina Supreme Court and involves a slip and fall at a local Walmart. In that case a bottle of olive oil was left broken in the aisle for three hours. The oil made the floor slippery. Walmart noted that the bottle and slippery condition was reported no less than fifteen times in the three-hour interval. A customer slipped on the oily floor resulting in a broken arm. The court found Walmart negligent and responsible for the cost of the injury. Case B is from the North Carolina Court of Appeals. In case B, a customer at a local Target store tripped over a toy truck spraining their ankle. The customer admitted placing the toy truck on the floor of the aisle to look at it from all angles. The court ruled in Target's favor finding no negligence on the store's part. Which case is precedent? Remember, precedent means cases with the same legal issue and same or similar factual predicate have the same outcomes. Case A and B both involve big box stores and slip and fall with resulting customer injuries. Case B differs in that it is the customer who created the circumstances resulting in the injury. In case A the store knew of the broken bottle of olive oil and did nothing to clean up the floor which ultimately resulted in the customer's injury. Case A is precedential. Case B is not. Case A involves the same legal issue as our Target example and the facts are similar. In the Target example and in case A the facts are similar. Both involve (1) a substance on the floor creating a slippery environment, (2) notice of the danger, (3) a failure to act to remedy the danger, and (4) an injury because of the danger. Our conclusion is same legal issue and same or similar facts so precedent.

Review What You've Read

1. In your own words, describe the importance of court hierarchy in determining precedent.

2. Name the sources of primary authority and why they qualify as primary authority.

3. Define weight in your own words.

4. Name two reasons secondary sources are valuable to the research process.

Chapter 2

Legal Analysis and Legal Research

Legal analysis is the application of the law to the facts of the controversy or matter to resolve the legal issue. Legal research is a process in which the researcher identifies the law or legal rules to support a legal argument or summary of the existing law. The legal research process is recursive, meaning you research, write, research more, and finalize your argument. The research process begins with an analysis of the facts and ends with the application of law to the facts. In legal research finding a case, statute, or regulation is step one of your research but never the last step.

Figure 2.1 Life Cycle of Legal Research

Once you locate a potentially relevant source you must analyze the source considering the following criteria:

1. Relevance
2. Type of authority

3. Weight of authority

4. Validity—if the source is law, is the law good law?

You will recognize the first three questions as the familiar questions from the decision tree in Chapter 1. Question 4 is new, asking that you validate your primary authority as good law using a citator. A thorough discussion of citators is found in Chapter 14.

It is key that you answer these four questions for each source you locate. Question 3 is familiar to you from the authority decision tree but should now be considered with the added complexities of the concept of precedent and the doctrine of stare decisis. Analysis of a case requires the researcher to consider the impact of precedent. Recall that the same or similar factual predicate combined with the same legal issue should produce the same result. Stare decisis obligates the court to apply a case as precedent when the case is from the same jurisdiction. Your analysis of an opinion for *relevance* should ask if the legal issues are the same. If the answer is no, you move on. If your answer is yes, then consider the facts. How similar are your facts to the ones in the opinion? Consider this as a continuum. The more the facts are alike, the stronger the fit. The less similar the facts, the greater the opportunity for you to *distinguish* the opinion from your matter. Distinguishing a case is to argue it lacks precedential value as the facts or legal issue are dissimilar. This suggests to the court that the existing opinion is sufficiently *not like* and so not precedent. This determination frees the court from the obligation to follow the existing result in this present instance.

An analogy is a comparison between two points for the purpose of explanation. In law we often argue by analogy when there is no relevant precedent. Your analysis of a source should identify points of similarity and difference for the purpose of creating your analogy.

Finding a source during the research process is merely the initial step in legal analysis. Evaluation of that source requires you to engage in analysis for fit for use to resolve your client's problem. Reflect on the tools you use in other courses like case briefs and IRAC, or Issue, Rule of law, Analysis, Conclusion. These common tools are methods of analysis. It is not enough to find a source. You must consider how you will use a source. You must engage in analysis to draw sound conclusions.

The following questions are useful in guiding your analysis by analogy or formulating a synthesized rule. These questions also permit you to determine a source's relevance and weight in your analysis.

- Does the source explain your legal concept?
- Does the source assist in identifying new legal vocabulary or legal jargon?
- Is the case factually analogous?
- Is this the leading case or the controlling statute?
- If the source is primary authority, does it provide a rule of law? If so, what is the rule of law? Apply your facts to the rule of law for fit.
- Does the source expand upon or revise a prior rule of law?
- Does the source provide a reference (i.e., a cross-reference) to another primary or secondary authority?
- Do you plan to use this source in your final work product? If so, how?

What is the conclusion you reach? Is your legal question answered? How is this specific opinion relevant to your research? Finding a relevant or good case is more than simply finding an opinion in a result set. To be relevant the case and specifically the holding must speak to the legal question. It is a case that may be cited as authority for the law. It is also a beginning as it can provide a link to additional cases that provide history and/or further development of a legal theory.

Review What You've Read

1. Describe, in your own words, the importance of relevance in the research process.

2. Name the four factors your analysis should address.

Chapter 3

Research Planning—
Creating a Research Strategy and
Documenting Your Research

Use the information you have. Understand the context of your search. Reliance on the Ouija board is never a good idea.[1]

The Research Plan

In its most simplistic form, a legal research plan is a strategy for finding information to advise your client with accurate solutions to their legal problems. Developing a strategy maximizes efficiency, effectiveness, and accuracy through a systematic approach to a problem rather than relying on luck. There is no single correct form of research plan. You will develop your own style of planning as you develop your preferred research methods. However, a defined strategy is essential to efficient, effective, and accurate research and stands in contrast to research that is merely a shot in the dark.

Stakes

1. You skip over the planning stage and begin researching by throwing random search terms into platform or database search box. You miss the controlling case because you've not focused your research.

2. You skip over the planning stage but successfully find the relevant, primary, binding authority. Unfortunately, your research was not efficient, and you billed three times the amount

---

1. *See generally* Robert Berring and Elizabeth A. Edinger, Finding the Law 87 (12th ed. 2005).

time to the file. Your senior partner is unhappy; the client refuses to pay the bill.

The research planning stage is brainstorming. You are not yet conducting research. Rather, you are gathering information and setting out a path to conduct your research. You are concentrating on your client's legal matter and, specifically, the facts (known and unknown) of that matter. What happened, where, when, and under what circumstances? What is the legal question involved? What is the client's desired outcome? Which types of legal information and what specific sources will help me to find the legal rules to answer the legal question for my client? How much time do I have? Have I applied the legal rule or rules to my legal issue to resolve the matter?

Elements of a Research Plan
I. Statement of the controlling jurisdiction
II. Identify legal question/Preliminary issue statement
III. List of the determinative facts
IV. Search terms and corresponding synonyms
V. Sources that are likely to contain helpful and relevant materials and an order in which you will use such sources.

A research plan consists of the determinative facts, an issue statement, identification of the controlling jurisdiction, search terms and alternatives, and identification of sources likely to contain the legal rules to solve your client's problem. In addition to these elements, you should also consider the pragmatic factors of your research. Such factors include time allotted to the project, the final product to be produced, and any limitation on use of resources.

Pragmatic Factors
1. Budget—time and money
2. End product—memo, brief, Zoom or conference call
3. Limitation on use of resources

The fact that these are pragmatic considerations does not diminish their importance. Resources have a cost, be it the cost to access a database on a platform like Westlaw[2] or Lexis or the cost of a firm to purchase

---

2. Westlaw Edge and Lexis + commonly and frequently change the name of their research platform to reflect the implementation of new functionality or design. The terms

a print copy of the state code. The cost of the resource is a consideration in the same way an attorney or client places a value on the research project itself. In addition to resources available through subscription platforms like Westlaw and Lexis, there are a number of free and low-cost resources available through the state bar associations and the internet. Evaluating the quality of these free resources is critical to efficient and effective research. Understanding that the U.S. Code available for free on https://govinfo.gov is an authenticated resource and the equivalent of the version in print in your library is key to effective resource selection of free resources. Likewise, the real world places restrictions on access to resources. It is not unheard of for a client or firm to limit access to Westlaw or Lexis. A well-conceived plan will acknowledge any such restrictions or concerns. An awareness of the client's desired result or endgame and the case of the opposition is also of significance in developing a strategy. It is not sufficient research to simply find the law that supports your client. A good lawyer understands and anticipates the opponent's case and is ready to address contrary authority.

Before you begin to develop a research plan, you must read the problem. Conduct a preliminary assessment of the problem. Highlight the jurisdiction, terms of art, who, what, where, when, the area of law, anything that looks like a determinative fact. Get a sense of the legal question presented. Read the following problem and then the annotated version illustrating an initial assessment of the problem.

Assessment of the Problem

Ritz Carlton Berne or "Bitzy" is an AKC-registered, prize-winning show dog. Charlie Murphy, Bitzy's owner, is devoted to him. She regularly breeds him for a stud fee reflecting his reputation as champion.

Each night around 5 PM, Charlie and Bitzy visit the dog park at the end of her street in Lewisburg, West Virginia. Charlie anticipates this nightly ritual. Bitzy is known to be well-mannered and play well with the other dogs. Charlie enjoys the break at the end of the day, visiting with the other dog lovers, and playing with Bitzy and generally taking a moment to pause and relax

---

Westlaw and Lexis are used herein to refer to the current instance of the database regardless of the current iteration of the name.

from her stressful day. About a month ago, a new arrival to the dog park began to spoil the fun nightly ritual. The new dog, a standard poodle named Bobo, disrupted Charlie's nightly ritual with his actions toward Bitzy and, by extension, Charlie. Bobo is highly aggressive and delights in lunging at the smaller dog. Bobo's owner, Ridley Scott, cannot control Bobo. Mr. Scott laughs off Bobo's behavior joking that he and Bobo flunked obedience class. He quickly follows up that Bobo is harmless, Bobo "wouldn't harm the fur on any dog's head." Multiple other owners frequenting the dog park have spoken to Scott repeatedly about Bobo's aggressive behavior. Scott's routine is to ignore the concern and reply, Bobo "hadn't bit anyone, yet."

Charlie began to skip her beloved nightly outing over anxiety at taking Bitzy to the dog park. She told fellow dog owner, June, she felt emotional distress at the thought of going to the dog park. Last Friday, she finally relented due to Bitzy's forlorn look at the door and leash. The inevitable happened. Upon Bitzy and Charlie's arrival at the dog park, Bobo grabbed Bitzy by the neck with his jaws firmly clasped around the scruff of Bitzy's neck violently shaking the smaller dog back and forth. Charlie was hysterical trying unsuccessfully to separate the two dogs. In this process, Charlie was seriously bitten by Bobo. Scott, after several feeble attempts, managed to get Bobo to drop Bitzy. The damage was done; Bitzy's neck was broken. When Charlie realized her dog was dead her hysterics increased; she clutched her chest and collapsed, unconscious. Paramedics were called and Charlie was transported to the local hospital where she was treated for a heart attack.

Charlie seeks your representation in an action against Ridley Scott.

Annotating Your Assessment of the Problem

Annotating the problem grounds you as the researcher. It is an entry point into the research query permitting you to dissect the problem in a contemplative manner. It asks you to think about what you need to know. Who am I representing? What is the issue and what are the determinative facts? Are there terms of art? What is the subject of the research? Where did the incident take place and what is the controlling jurisdiction? When did the incident occur and is there a time frame for my research? Why am I researching this? What is it I need to accomplish? What is my end product? It is thorough reading and contemplation of the problem.

The following image illustrates an initial reading of the problem highlighting and annotating relevant features like jurisdiction, potentially determinative facts, causes of action, terms of art. It is an initial pass on the problem.

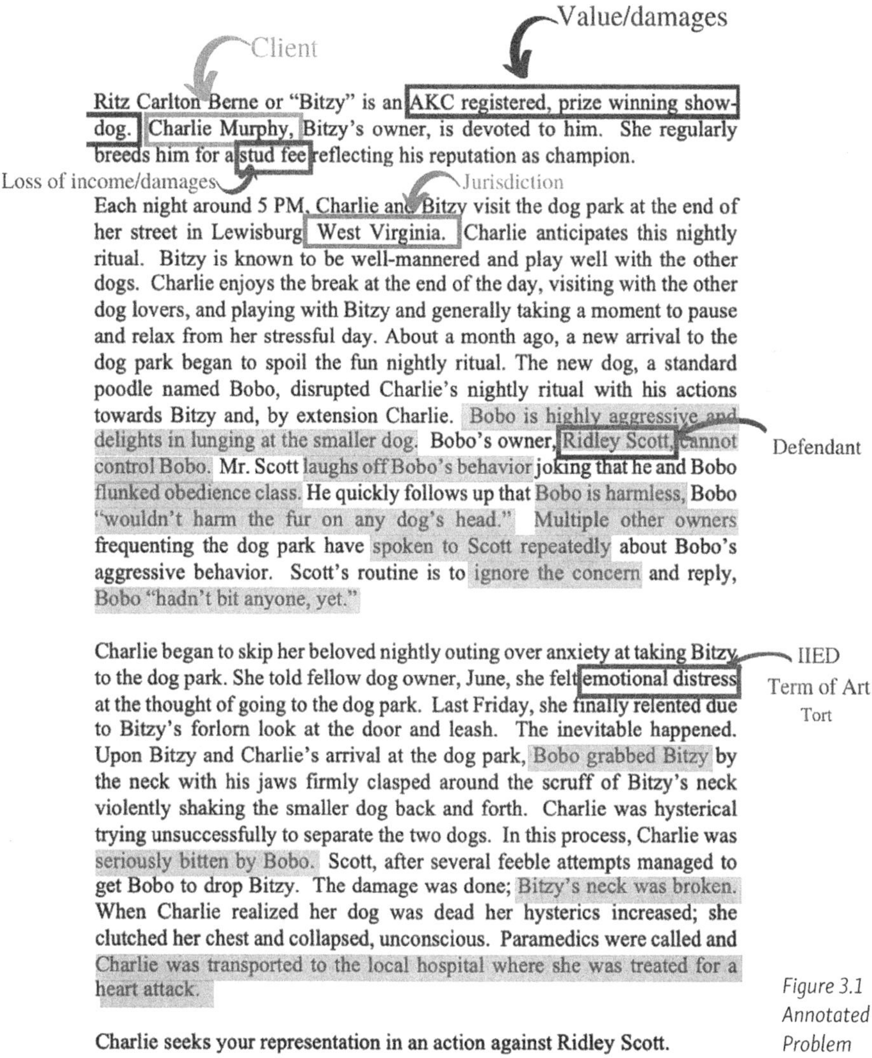

Value/damages

Client

Ritz Carlton Berne or "Bitzy" is an AKC registered, prize winning show-dog. Charlie Murphy, Bitzy's owner, is devoted to him. She regularly breeds him for a stud fee reflecting his reputation as champion.

Loss of income/damages

Jurisdiction

Each night around 5 PM, Charlie and Bitzy visit the dog park at the end of her street in Lewisburg West Virginia. Charlie anticipates this nightly ritual. Bitzy is known to be well-mannered and play well with the other dogs. Charlie enjoys the break at the end of the day, visiting with the other dog lovers, and playing with Bitzy and generally taking a moment to pause and relax from her stressful day. About a month ago, a new arrival to the dog park began to spoil the fun nightly ritual. The new dog, a standard poodle named Bobo, disrupted Charlie's nightly ritual with his actions towards Bitzy and, by extension Charlie. Bobo is highly aggressive and delights in lunging at the smaller dog. Bobo's owner, Ridley Scott, cannot control Bobo. Mr. Scott laughs off Bobo's behavior joking that he and Bobo flunked obedience class. He quickly follows up that Bobo is harmless, Bobo "wouldn't harm the fur on any dog's head." Multiple other owners frequenting the dog park have spoken to Scott repeatedly about Bobo's aggressive behavior. Scott's routine is to ignore the concern and reply, Bobo "hadn't bit anyone, yet."

Defendant

Charlie began to skip her beloved nightly outing over anxiety at taking Bitzy to the dog park. She told fellow dog owner, June, she felt emotional distress at the thought of going to the dog park. Last Friday, she finally relented due to Bitzy's forlorn look at the door and leash. The inevitable happened. Upon Bitzy and Charlie's arrival at the dog park, Bobo grabbed Bitzy by the neck with his jaws firmly clasped around the scruff of Bitzy's neck violently shaking the smaller dog back and forth. Charlie was hysterical trying unsuccessfully to separate the two dogs. In this process, Charlie was seriously bitten by Bobo. Scott, after several feeble attempts managed to get Bobo to drop Bitzy. The damage was done; Bitzy's neck was broken. When Charlie realized her dog was dead her hysterics increased; she clutched her chest and collapsed, unconscious. Paramedics were called and Charlie was transported to the local hospital where she was treated for a heart attack.

IED
Term of Art
Tort

Figure 3.1
Annotated
Problem

Charlie seeks your representation in an action against Ridley Scott.

Step 1: The Issue Statement

Creating an *issue statement,* also referred to as the *question present-ed,* focuses your research. It is a statement of the legal question or legal issue the court must decide. Correct identification of the legal issue is essential. It is common for a research question to have multiple issues or sub-issues. When you formulate a preliminary statement of the problem you define the scope of the research problem. The act of constructing the hypothesis or issue statement usually requires some knowledge of the relevant law that you may or may not have in the brainstorming phase of your research. As you research, you may refine the issue statement based on a new or better understanding of the problem. Framing the initial statement should not be confused with constructing the finely honed question presented for a brief or memo, but rather is a first draft. Research the correct issue and not the issue you prefer. Do not be afraid to reconsider the initial question. What you find may impact how you view the initial issue statement and suggest refinement or change.

Your issue statement should have three distinct parts:

- Part 1—the controlling jurisdiction
- Part 2—the legal question
- Part 3—the determinative facts

i. Statement of Jurisdiction

The United States is composed of fifty-one-plus jurisdictions. Given the importance of precedent and stare decisis in our system, identifica-tion of the controlling jurisdiction is necessary. It helps you to frame the legal information you find through the research process in the context of legal authority.

Identification of the appropriate jurisdiction aids you in identifying controlling from persuasive authority and restricts the universe of infor-mation. Research is expensive. An attorney's time, as well as the cost of accessing materials, is a crucial factor. The goal of a research project is always to locate all relevant authority. This includes authority that sup-ports your position as well as any that does not. Persuasive authority is often a luxury that cannot be afforded. What is the budget for your research? As an attorney's time has a value and client's pocketbooks are not unlimited, you must be aware of the cost of research. Understanding when you need to buttress an argument with persuasive authority is important. If the matter is one of clearly settled law, locating the binding authority is usually sufficient. If the matter is one of first impression, spending the time and resources to locate persuasive, primary authority from jurisdictions that have addressed the matter or locating law review articles or other secondary sources that opine on the topic may be a wise investment.

The controlling jurisdiction refers to the source of binding authority and is distinct from venue, which is where a case may be filed or tried. Identification of the controlling jurisdiction in a research plan is usually a single phrase. Is the issue federal or state? If federal, which appellate circuit? If state, which state and does the state have an intermediate appellate court with associated districts or circuits? Therefore, a simple statement such as: Federal, Fourth Circuit for a federal issue, or North Carolina for a state law matter is usually sufficient. If there are multiple issues, be cautious to determine if there are different jurisdictions. Remember the federal courts are their own, separate jurisdiction.

ii. The Legal Question

Identification of the legal question asks you to articulate the legal question to be resolved in your own words. The legal question you are researching is the foundation of a research project. This is the initial identification of the legal issue or legal question to be researched.

iii. Determining Your Legally Relevant Facts

Not all facts are *legally relevant*. Legally relevant facts, or determinative facts, are facts upon which the answer to a legal question will turn. If a fact, when altered, changes the answer to the legal question or outcome of the case, then it is a determinative fact. Your research plan should contain a summary or list of determinative facts. Exclude facts that are explanatory in nature or circumstantial. Your goal is to sort through the facts provided to identify only those that are determinative and relevant to the legal question at hand. Do not copy and paste paragraphs of facts to into your research plan. That defeats the purpose and avoids a critical step of analysis. You must cull the facts and consider those that are relevant and those that are not to create your list of determinative facts. Do not omit facts that are legally relevant but unfavorable. Determinative facts do not include legal conclusions. You may find it helpful to draft a timeline of the events. Identify each person involved and their place in the controversy. Evaluate the importance of each fact and what value or function is served. Consider these questions to help assess each fact:

1. Does the fact identify a cause of action?
2. Does the fact identify the jurisdiction?
3. Does the outcome of the matter depend upon this fact?
4. Does the answer to the legal question depend upon this fact?

Develop a clear understanding of the factual predicate of your argument. Understanding the facts assists you in focusing your research.

Construction of the Issue Statement [3]

Under [controlling law], does [legal question], when [determinative facts]?

Whether [legal question], under [controlling law], when [determinative facts].

One common formulation of an issue statement is the *under, does, when* formulation. Under *[applicable law]*, does[4] *[legal question]*, when *[determinative facts]*. Think back to our slip-and-fall example.

> *I am in a Target store in Charlotte, North Carolina when I slip and fall due to someone who left a leaky bottle of oil on the floor. The manager of the store was informed of the presence of the spill where it remained for several hours before I slipped and fell due to the oil resulting in injury.*

A complete issue statement for the slip-and-fall matter might look like:

---

3. Christine Coughlin et al., A Lawyer Writes A Practical Guide to Legal Analysis 219 (2d ed. 2013).

4. It is appropriate to consider when the action took place and adjust the language. *Does* may become *is, did,* or *would.*

Under North Carolina law, does one incur liability for negligence, when a bottle of spilled baby oil is left on the floor of a large store creating a slippery floor and a visitor to the store falls due to the spilled oil resulting in injury?

The issue statement is a single sentence. Accordingly, preliminary issue statements often break the rules for run-on sentences. An issue statement may be three or four lines. This is the one time in your life when it is okay to be wordy. Still, your issue statement should be as concise as possible and easily understandable. Note what is not included in an issue statement:

- Proper names of clients—instead opt for a generic descriptor.
- Do not assume away the answer to the legal question with a legal conclusion.
- Copy and paste of sentences is not appropriate for an issue statement.

Step 2: Generating Search Terms

A search term is an expression of the concept you intend to research. Search terms describe the factual situation and the legal question at hand. Your search terms are also the building blocks of terms and connector or Boolean search statements. Often, identifying good search terms is the most difficult step of the planning stage. Online searching is powerful and a staple of the modern lawyer, when used correctly. Effective searches are central to efficient research. This section of the plan assists you in constructing a good search rather than merely throwing words at the wall to see what sticks. Full text searching, for all its attendant benefits, also has detriments. Consider the instance in which the controlling case is not located because the search involved the word "cat" rather than "feline." Synonyms and concepts are critical to good research. Generating a list of search terms should also consider phrases designed to locate legal concepts or theories. Often legal concepts are best located through phrases rather than words. Start with the basic terms and phrases then expand by adding synonyms and antonyms. A good dictionary and thesaurus are also useful tools to consult when compiling a list. Use of a free online thesaurus is an excellent tool to generate synonyms and antonyms. Familiarity with the topic is always helpful. Lawyers and legal publishers love legal jargon. Failure to identifying the buzzwords, or jargon, or terms of art may mean you are never able to locate the results you seek. If you are not familiar with the topic, you are likely to find yourself revising your plan as you gain familiarity through secondary sources and your evaluation of relevant authorities. This is the planning process. Nothing is set in stone. Expect your research to be fluid, adjusting as you acquire knowledge.

Your search terms will evolve as you begin researching and gain a better understanding of the problem and the authorities. Taking a moment to consider the terms you think a judge, a legislature, or an agency might use when discussing the law you seek is key. Judges tend to write as we do. In contrast, legislators and persons who draft rules tend to think and write in highly technical and prescriptive terms in crafting the language of a statute or regulation. Understanding the author will help you anticipate the language used in the case, statute, or regulation and inform your search terms. As you develop your search terms, think about the legal concepts involved, the generic version of the facts, and the language a court, legislature, or agency might use. Examples of legal terms of art[5] include *res ipsa*, *mens rea*, *proximate cause*, *noncompete clause* these are considered terms of art because they have a special meaning in law. Think about synonyms, antonyms, and alternative words the author might use to describe the matter. There are multiple models that may assist in developing search terms. Commonly used prompts for search terms include the W questions borrowed from journalists; PPT, or people, places, things; and TARPP, or things, actions, remedies people, place. See Appendix B for the common prompts for search terms. Use the prompt that you find fits either the question or your comfort level.

Some things are not properly classified as search terms. Jurisdiction is an obvious example. West Virginia, North Carolina, or Georgia as jurisdiction is not appropriately included as a response to the *where* of the W question, or *place* in PPT or TARPP. Jurisdiction is appropriately addressed by using a filter rather than inclusion as a search term.

---

5. Term of art—a phrase with a specialized meaning in a particular field.

Models to Develop Search Terms	
W questions	Who, what, where, when, and why
PPT	People, places, things
TARPP	Things, actions, remedies, people, place

Figure 3.2 Models to Develop Search Terms[6]

There is no right or wrong in selection of the model. One may appeal to you more than another. Use the one that provides you the greatest comfort.

Once you identify a term, you must then identify alternative terms and synonyms. You take this step as courts and legislatures do not adopt uniform language. It is important to understand there are multiple ways and words that may be used to describe similar things.

Continuing with our slip-and-fall example, the completed *W* prompt might look like:

Prompt — unique search term — alternative terms and synonyms

Who — shopper — consumer, visitor, guest

What — fall — trip, slip, spill

Where — store — premises, aisle, stadium

When — "business hours" — day time, evening, open

Why — injury — damage, hurt, impaired

Remember your goal in identifying search terms is to think about the terms that will appear in a relevant document. Find terms that are descriptive but not factually distinct. Consider what is not included in the example above:

- Proper names—Jan, Marcia, Greg, or your client's name is not useful so, as with the issue statement, avoid proper names in favor of a generic descriptor.

---

6. *See* Appendix B for the templates associated with these prompts.

- North Carolina—avoid the jurisdiction or specific place names like Target. What if the best case on your facts involves Walmart?
- 5PM or a specific time. The *when* question is a temporal question. It may or may not be relevant given your specific question.

Step 3: Search Statements

Some may elect to take an additional step of writing out the intended search. This is particularly useful when using Boolean or terms and connectors searches. Seeing a search in writing can help you consider how the search terms relate to each other. Even those using natural language search methodology may benefit from seeing the query prior to running the search. The value of writing out the search is in seeing it and considering exactly what you have instructed the research platform to retrieve in a search. This simple concept—understanding what you have instructed the research platform to do—requires some familiarity with how a platform processes a search, which is explored in detail in Part III.

Step 4: Identification of Useful Sources and the Order in Which They Are to Be Accessed

Once you identify the issue and the jurisdiction, the next step is to identify potentially useful sources and order of intended use. You seek to identify sources likely to contain relevant information based upon your understanding of the types of legal information available to you. Establish a plan by listing the sources that you believe will contain the authority sought. Once you have a list, consider the order in which you plan to access them. Your order should reflect a logic building from one resource to the next. For example, you are given a statutory citation as part of the information on your legal question. In this example you would list the code you will use to find the statute. The code would be assigned a *1* on your list of potential sources. From there you might use the annotations in the code to locate judicial opinions that interpret the statute. Caselaw from the controlling jurisdiction would be assigned a *2* on your list. You might list a treatise or legal encyclopedia as *3* or *4* based upon your understanding and familiarity with the topic. This is brainstorming, so names of sources may vary from generic, a state legal encyclopedia, to specific, the North Carolina code, based on your familiarity with the sources. Your objective here is to brainstorm which source is likely to have the information you want, not to memorialize the perfect name.

As a researcher, you look for authority to support the argument to be made on behalf of your client. Questions of what types of authorities are sought, why the type of authority is helpful, and where it may be located are central to this part of the plan. Secondary sources are particularly effective in assisting in the understanding of the actual problem and the location of primary authorities.

Remember this is brainstorming. Your list of sources will likely deviate and evolve as you begin researching. This step is intended to establish an informed starting point. This portion of the plan is often the most fluid. Identification of initial sources frequently expands to include other sources as the material is located. It is not a linear process. Inherently the research process is circular. It involves finding information, making a judgment call concerning the utility of such information, and then refining your plan. It is expected you will revisit areas of the plan or strategy the more you learn. You may add or delete search terms or entire issues as well as identify new issues, search terms, and sources of interest.

The customary goal of research is to locate the binding or mandatory, primary authority that answers your legal question. This requires locating the case, statute, rule, and/or regulation addressing the issue from the relevant jurisdiction. Secondary authorities are useful tools to educate a researcher on a topic. They assist in developing search terms and a basic understanding of the concept. Finding aids, citators, and secondary authorities all aid in the identification of primary authorities.

Persuasive authorities also assist in refining or buttressing an argument and more specifically in the instance of a case of first impression. Before one spends a client's time and money on locating persuasive authority, consider the question of why it is necessary. Is this a case of first impression (i.e., no governing rule exists in the controlling jurisdiction)? Does your argument depend on the use of an analogy to support your reasoning? Do you need to support your position with additional cases? Each is a valid reason to support the search for additional authority;

however, always consider the pragmatic parameters of the project. Law school invites the all-encompassing or mega-search for authority. The real world of practice includes fiscal and temporal constraints. The ultimate question to ask is: does the client benefit from the time spent locating persuasive authority? Finally, is the authority located correctly identified as persuasive rather than mandatory?

The order in which you elect to use resources will contribute to your efficiency. What source do I use as a starting point? Where do I go from there? Your goal is to build on the information you find from one source to the next. There is no one correct starting point for a research project. The answer to "where do I begin?" depends upon what you have and know. When brainstorming sources and the order in which you will use them, your goal is to have a logical order in which you use the sources, and you should focus on the goal of locating primary, binding authority.

Where Do I Begin?	
I have background knowledge on my topic	Build on that knowledge with primary sources.
I was given a source as a starting point	Begin with that source and build from there. For example, if you are given an opinion, you should read the opinion for relevance and then use the tools you will discover in our search strategies to build from there.
I know nothing about this area of law	Begin with a secondary source. This will provide a general understanding of the area, educate you on the legal jargon or vocabulary unique to the areal of law, and provide research references to primary and other secondary authorities.
I was given a statute from a non-controlling jurisdiction	This is usually not a useful starting point as it lacks the analysis or explanation of a secondary authority and is not controlling authority. If it is all you have, you may use the subject matter of the statute to find an on-point topic or key number (*see search strategies*) or employ a citator (*see search strategies*) to assist but this is your least promising starting point.

Figure 3.3 Where Do I Begin?

Today's research environment has a foot in both the print and online worlds. Complete, accurate, and efficient research generally requires use of both free and subscription sources, as well as print. Do not conflate the use of free source as equivalent to cost-effective research. Your time is valuable and repeating a search originally done on Google in Westlaw or Lexis when you could have simply done the search in Westlaw or Lexis is inefficient. Some find statutory research to be easier to conduct in print, especially when the research is historical. Each will find their own path as there is no single correct path.

Efficiency and accuracy are the identifiable benefits to creating and following a strategy, methodology, or plan. Taking the time to create a plan and organize your thoughts increases both the efficiency and the accuracy of the search. Planning minimizes the risk that important authorities are missed. The adage "time is money" is especially true for lawyers. Research is expensive. It takes time to do quality analysis and research and the rate for a billable hour is anything but cheap. Resources also have associated costs. This requires attorneys to be efficient and accurate. A research plan avoids the haphazard search that often misses important authorities and ensures that all the key sources necessary to locate relevant authorities are searched. The bonus of planning a strategy is confidence in the process.

Time to Stop or Revisit

I've found the universe of resources on my topic when I am finding the same sources again and again.

When have I found my answer? More commonly the question is: when am I finished with my research? Research and writing have a symbiotic relationship. You research to know the law, develop a position and argument, and formulate the best advice for your client. You write to convey the law to another. Too often research and writing are viewed as separate processes that fail to connect. This is a mistake. The processes are intertwined in the most basic sense. The attorney conceives the initial argument and then must locate the authorities to support that position. As they research, they refine the argument based on the actual law. The process is symbiotic: research, write, refine, write, and research until the final product is completed. This does not address the question of when I am finished. Knowing when to stop is influenced by factors such as repetitive findings of the same sources or the failure to locate anything. Both indicate a need to stop. The difficulty in providing a definitive answer to this question is that there is often not a definitive answer to the legal question. In matters involving a novel question of law or a matter of first impression you are likely to be constructing an argument by analogy. When you find that you are locating the same sources repeatedly, you are likely to have discovered the universe of law relating to your question. At that point you have located the relevant sources and are *finished*. In the alternative, if you think that your question is not answered, it is time to revisit your search strategy and plan and refine.

Stakes

When you use WAZE to get directions from point A to point B, you make choices about the route. You may elect to avoid toll roads or highways. You can choose fast or slow. You make choices based on the circumstances. The order in which you elect to use research sources is also like choosing a route to navigate from point A to point B. Using sources in a logical and thoughtful manner will result in efficient and effective results and appropriate use of your time. If you merely jump from one source to another with no clear path or purpose, you are likely to either miss a key source resulting in a loss for your client and/or run up a large bill that your client refuses to pay.

Documenting Your Research—The Research Log

You have your plan. Now put your plan into action. As you research, you will want to keep a record of what you find. Revisit your strategy and revise as needed should your initial plan fail to produce the expected results. As you build your argument, you will find gaps that need to be filled, requiring additional research. For all these reasons it is helpful to maintain a record of your research efforts. Many use the folder system and the research trails available on Westlaw, Lexis, and Bloomberg Law to fill this function. These are excellent tools that facilitate sharing with colleagues and include automatic updates of citator flags but are limited to their research platforms. Note-taking must be comprehensive.

The research log is one tool many find useful in documenting your research progress. Suppose another attorney must take over the case or the case file needs to be updated? Another attorney can see your work to date and continue your work or update the results. If your answer is "I cannot find an answer," you need to be able to show documentation of your research process to date. The research log is a comprehensive list of the sources found summarizing the findings. There are many ways to log your progress. A template of the log is found in Appendix E.

A research log documents the sources found while executing your research plan. Your log will include sources of varying degrees of relevance and utility. It is a record of your work. Each log entry describes the source and evaluates it on a number of important criteria. Use the blank template of the research log to complete research exercises along with the "Instructions for Completing a Research Log" provided.

Source 1:	*Source citation:*	
	Authority:	Type of authority:
		Weight of authority:
	Description of search:	Search strategy:
		Description of steps taken:
	Currency:	
	Validity:	
	Analyze the authority: (Choose the relevant prompts from the instructions to answer thoroughly)	

Figure 3.4 Research Log Block Template

A minimal amount of information is required to make the log useful when needed; however, the researcher may make the log as detailed a summary of the research process as desired. The goal is to provide sufficient detail to return to the source. At a minimum, you should document the following information:

- Citation
- Type of authority—primary or secondary
- Weight of authority—binding/mandatory or non-binding/ persuasive
- Where/how found—your search strategy, the terms and connectors statement used, any pre-search and post-search filters employed. What worked and what did not?
- Currency—"current" is insufficient. A date or reference to a point in time reflects currency.
- Validity—Validity is a question for primary authorities. Is the law good law?
- Analysis of authority for utility and relevance.

Review What You've Read

1. What are the three search prompts for identifying search terms?

2. What are the five elements of a research plan?

3. What are the pragmatic factors of a research plan?

4. What makes a fact a determinative fact?

Chapter 4

Legal Citation

Why do we need to cite?
The judge does not trust you, not one scintilla.[1]

Think of legal citation as providing an address. In law we tell the opposing counsel and the judge where to find the authority we are citing. In effect, we give an address to where the language we are using can be found. The legal citation also provides information about the source. The educated reader can quickly determine if the source is primary or secondary, binding or nonbinding, by simply reading the citation. *The Bluebook: A Uniform System of Citation,* commonly known as *The Bluebook*, is the common source for legal citation although there are others including *ALWD Guide to Legal Citation* and *The Greenbook.* A quick glance at an unopened *Bluebook* suggests the complexity associated with legal citation. The rules are detailed. The good news is that legal citation is formulaic and once you master a few rules it becomes repetitive. There are two guidelines to keep in mind. First, copy and paste is not your friend and it is particularly terrible with secondary source citations. Westlaw, Lexis and other research platforms and databases cannot be relied upon for correct citation format—online or in print. One glaring example is the correct abbreviation for Michie's Jurisprudence, the Virginia/West Virginia legal encyclopedia. Michie's Jurisprudence is correctly abbreviated as Michie's. Jur. not M.J. as it appears on Lexis. Second, citation is important because it is a quick assessment by the reader of the quality of your work. Well-cited work reflects positively on well-written substance.

---

1. Anonymous 1L professor at Washington & Lee University School of Law (Spring 2017).

Practice Tip

Sometimes the Bluebook lacks a definitive example or explanation as to how to cite a source. When in doubt, search the Harvard L. Rev. on Westlaw, Lexis, or HeinOnline for an example of a citation to that source. Harvard Law Review editors are among the editors of the Bluebook. Seeing how they cited the item in doubt is a good way to find a reliable example for a correct citation.

Templates for Common Citations According to *The Bluebook*

All references to Rules are to The Bluebook
#—indicates a space

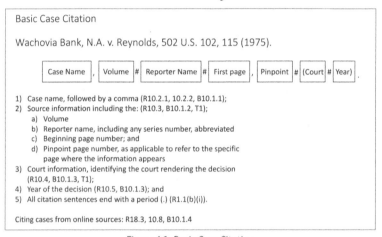

Figure 4.1 Basic Case Citation

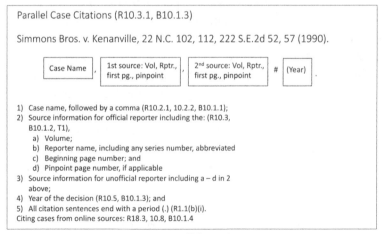

Figure 4.2 Parallel Case Citations

The need for parallel citation is determined by local court rules. Many courts have moved away from requiring parallel citations. Confirm with the court if parallel cites are required by local rules.

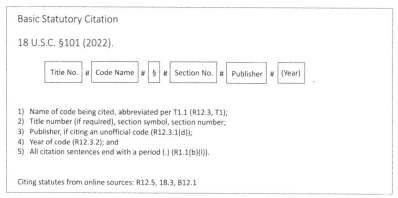

Figure 4.3 Basic Statutory Citation

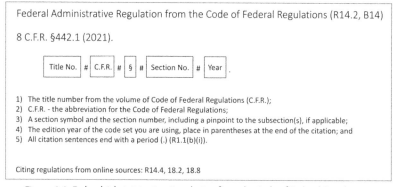

Figure 4.4 Federal Administrative Regulation from the Code of Federal Regulations

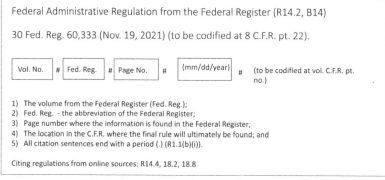

Figure 4.5 Federal Administrative Regulation from the Federal Register

Treatises or Books
Rod Smolla, *The First Amendment* 614 (3rd ed. 2022).

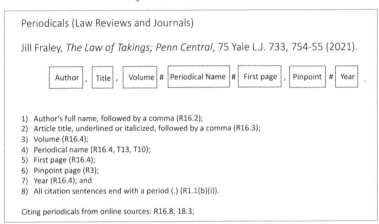

1) Author's full name, followed by a comma (R15.1);
2) Book title, underlined or italicized (R15.3);
3) Pinpoint page(s) or section(s) (R3);
4) Publication edition, or other information if applicable (R15.2, 15.4);
5) Year of publication (R15.4); and
6) All citation sentences end with a period (.) (R1.1(b)(i)).

Citing treatises and books from online sources: R15.9, 18.2.2, 18.3

Figure 4.6 Treatises or Books

Periodicals (Law Reviews and Journals)

Jill Fraley, *The Law of Takings; Penn Central*, 75 Yale L.J. 733, 754-55 (2021).

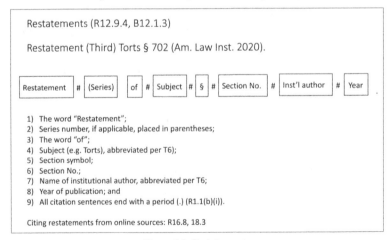

1) Author's full name, followed by a comma (R16.2);
2) Article title, underlined or italicized, followed by a comma (R16.3);
3) Volume (R16.4);
4) Periodical name (R16.4, T13, T10);
5) First page (R16.4);
6) Pinpoint page (R3);
7) Year (R16.4); and
8) All citation sentences end with a period (.) (R1.1(b)(i)).

Citing periodicals from online sources: R16.8, 18.3;

Figure 4.7 Periodicals (Law Reviews and Journals)

Restatements (R12.9.4, B12.1.3)

Restatement (Third) Torts § 702 (Am. Law Inst. 2020).

1) The word "Restatement";
2) Series number, if applicable, placed in parentheses;
3) The word "of";
4) Subject (e.g. Torts), abbreviated per T6);
5) Section symbol;
6) Section No.;
7) Name of institutional author, abbreviated per T6;
8) Year of publication; and
9) All citation sentences end with a period (.) (R1.1(b)(i)).

Citing restatements from online sources: R16.8, 18.3

Figure 4.8 Restatements

American Law Reports (R16.7.6)

Susan Miller, Annotation, *The Hidden Commerce Clause*, 3 A.L.R. Fed. 3d 103, 103 (2022).

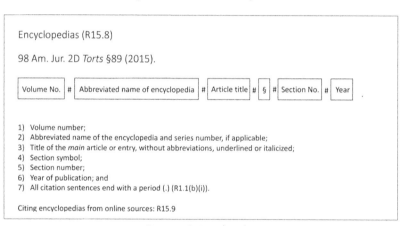

1) Author's full name including designations such as Jr. or III, but omitting terms such as Prof. or J.D., followed by a comma;
2) The word "Annotation", followed by a comma;
3) Title of the annotation, underlined or italicized, with no abbreviations. Capitalize the first letter of each word except articles, conjunctions, and prepositions, followed by a comma;
4) Volume number;
5) Abbreviation for American Law Reports (A.L.R.), followed by the series number (e.g., 5th, 6th, Fed.);
6) First page;
7) Pinpoint page;
8) Year of publications; and
9) All citation sentences end with a period (.) (R1.1(b)(i)).

Citing ALR from online sources: R16.8

Figure 4.9 American Law Reports

Encyclopedias (R15.8)

98 Am. Jur. 2D *Torts* §89 (2015).

| Volume No. | # | Abbreviated name of encyclopedia | # | Article title | # | § | # | Section No. | # | Year |

1) Volume number;
2) Abbreviated name of the encyclopedia and series number, if applicable;
3) Title of the *main* article or entry, without abbreviations, underlined or italicized;
4) Section symbol;
5) Section number;
6) Year of publication; and
7) All citation sentences end with a period (.) (R1.1(b)(i)).

Citing encyclopedias from online sources: R15.9

Figure 4.10 Encyclopedias

Review What You've Read—
Summary Part I

1. Name the four main sources of law.

2. In your own words, describe what is meant by the dual court system. Why is it important to understand the hierarchy of the court issuing an opinion?

3. Define the concepts of precedent and stare decisis.

4. Define each of the following types of authority, making it clear how each category is distinct from the other.

   a. Primary authority

   b. Secondary authority

   c. Persuasive authority

   d. Mandatory authority

5. Describe, in your own words, weight of authority.

6. What are the three components of an issue statement?

7. What makes a fact a *determinative fact* or a *legally relevant fact*?

8. Describe the steps in a research plan.

9. What is the distinction between a *search term* and a *research issue*?

Part II

The Sources of Legal Research

The universe of legal information which includes statements of the law, explanations, commentary on the law, and finding aids is vast. Legal sources exist in print and online for free and by subscription. Navigating these resources uses a plethora of skills and search strategies. Identifying a source, understanding its substance, its relevance, or how it adds value to your research, and knowing how to effectively navigate and use the source to answer a legal question are skills imperative to legal research and the practice of law.

LEARNING OBJECTIVES

- Distinguish between and identify different types of primary and secondary sources.
- Recognize when to utilize a specific type of source.
- Identify the authoritative or persuasive value of a source (weight).
- Understand the publication process of a source to distinguish between the versions for appropriate use.
- Identify the currency of a source.
- Assess the validity of a source.

Part II of this text discusses primary and secondary sources common to the legal research process. Primary sources, such as judicial opinions, statutes, constitutions, and regulations are discussed in detail. Similarly, the specific legal research sources that explain the law, including the secondary sources of legal encyclopedia, American Law Reports, Restatements, legal periodicals, and treatises, are detailed. Finally, the special tools that help us navigate and use sources, also known as *finding aids* such as *Words and Phrases* and digests, are considered.

Chapter 5

The Judicial Opinion

Characteristics of the Judicial Opinion

1. Primary authority.
2. May constitute binding, mandatory, or controlling authority or non-binding or persuasive, primary authority.
3. Issued by a judicial branch in its law-making capacity.
4. The holding constitutes precedent.

Judges from any of the courts in any of the fifty-one federal and state court systems issue written decisions in resolution of a matter before that court. Those decisions are law. We use judicial opinions:

1. To interpret, understand, or explain legislation.
2. To interpret, understand, or explain regulations.
3. To locate the common law.

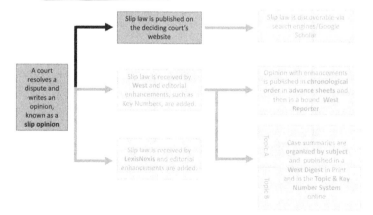

Figure 5.1 Publication Process of a Judicial Opinion—Slip Opinion

A judicial opinion is first published as a *slip opinion*. This is a document filed by the court with the clerk of court. These days the slip opinion is routinely made available via the court website. The slip opinion has no value-added research tools or other editorial content to help researchers interpret or use the opinion. These research tools are added later in the publication process by commercial publishers. The slip opinion is located using a docket number rather than the reporter citation. A docket number is the internal filing number of the court assigned to the matter and permits a researcher to locate any document associated with the matter at the court. The docket number is assigned to all documents of the matter. Slip opinions are then collected and published chronologically in volumes of sets called Reporters. For example, the Federal Reporter contains the decisions of the Federal Courts of Appeals, the West Virginia Reporter contains the decisions of the West Virginia Supreme Court of Appeals. The legal citation of a case is the reporter citation. It is effectively an address descriptive of the authority of the opinion, as the citation indicates the hierarchy and jurisdiction of the court.

Researchers should also note the distinction between an opinion of the court and an order. Trial courts often conclude a matter with an order rather than a written opinion. Orders dispose of the matter before the court but are not an opinion of the court.

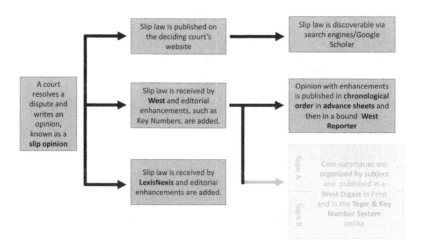

Figure 5.2 Publication Process of a Judicial Opinion—Advance Sheets

For some reporter series, the second instance of publication of a judicial opinion is the inclusion of the opinion in *advance sheets*. Advance sheets are the temporary publication of collections of recent opinions with editorial or research enhancement features circulated prior to inclusion in a reporter. The publication is temporary, as once the reporter volume containing the opinions is published the advance sheets are discarded. Advance sheets traditionally are published in pamphlet format and shelved at the end of the reporter collection.[1]

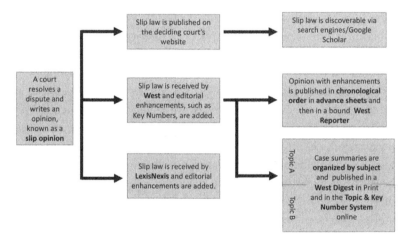

Figure 5.3 Publication Process of a Judicial Opinion—Reporter/Digest

The final step in the publication of a judicial opinion is its appearance in the print reporter. This is the final version that includes editorial or research enhancements. Reports publish cases designated by the court for publication in chronological order. Reporters may be geographic in their collection, publishing only the opinions of a court like the United States Reports publishing the opinions of the United States Supreme Court or they may be topical. For example, the United States Bankruptcy Reporter publishes decisions involving bankruptcy.

---

1. In 2022 Thomson Reuters ceased publication of advance sheets to selected reporters. This is likely the beginning of a trend to phase out publication of advance sheets.

Characteristics of a Reporter

1. Publishes judicial opinions in chronological order
2. Limited to a specific geographic designation or a specific court
3. May be designated as official or unofficial

Official vs. Unofficial and Precedential vs. Non-Precedential

Reporters are classified as *official* or *unofficial*. A reporter published pursuant to governmental authority is classified as an official reporter. Publication under specific governmental authority includes when a government authority designates a commercial publisher as the publisher. Commercial versus government publisher is not relevant; so long as the government arranges for the publication, the designation of official attaches. Conversely, publication by a commercial publisher such as West or Lexis in the absence of an official designation by the government authority results in an unofficial reporter designation. Regardless of the designation of official or unofficial, the underlying text of the opinion, the law itself, is the same. Opinions published in multiple reporters have multiple addresses. These are called parallel citations that document the multiple places an opinion may be located.

Reporter Specific Vocabulary	
National Reporter System	The unofficial reporters published by West/Thomson Reuters with decisions from United States jurisdictions.
Regional Reporter	State judicial opinions published by West/Thomson Reuters into seven distinct regions of the United States.

Figure 5.4 Reporter Specific Vocabulary

The unpublished or non-precedential opinion is an opinion not designated for publication by the court. Courts designate an opinion for publication, or not, at the point of issuance. Typically, only those opinions with substantive discussion of issues of law are designated for publication. Put another way, opinions that address issues of settled law are more likely to fall into the category of "not designated for publication." Only a fraction of judicial opinions is designated for publication. It is exclusively those opinions that appear in *print*. Prior to the explosion of online resources, an opinion not designated for publication was difficult to obtain. Such opinions existed exclusively in the file at the clerk of court's office. This difficulty of accessing such opinions is known as practical obscurity. Beginning in 2001, West/Thomson Reuters began collecting the unpublished decisions from the clerk of courts offices and publishing such opinions in the *Federal Appendix*. Thus, *unpublished* opinions were published appearing in print but lacking the weight of a published opinion. The looming question was: what is the precedential value of an unpublished decision? The significance of this question expanded as the volume of *unpublished* opinions increased in availability due to their inclusion in online research platforms such as Westlaw, Lexis, databases, or the internet. The availability of the opinion either in a print reporter or online begs the accuracy of the term *unpublished opinion*. The more accurate term to refer to these opinions is the term *non-precedential* opinion or non-precedential decision.

Non-precedential decisions refer to the value of an unpublished opinion in the terms of precedence. The unpublished opinion is often subject to specific court rules that dictate if, when, and under what circumstances an unpublished opinion might be cited to a court as authority. At the federal level this question was specifically addressed by an amendment to the Federal Rules of Appellate Procedure. Effective January 1, 2007, a non-precedential decision issued on or after January 1, 2007, may be cited to a federal court.[2] The rules governing the use of a non-precedential decisions vary at the state level and a prudent researcher will confirm the status with the applicable court rule.

The unresolved question regarding the authoritative value of the non-precedential decision. At best, the decision is persuasive. There may be inherent value in the non-precedential decision as a research tool.

Parts of Judicial Opinions

Judicial opinions are formulaic. They contain standard parts that are identifiable and individually searchable in databases in online research platforms. There are six parts of the judicial opinion.

---

2. FED. R. APP. P. 32.1.

Six Parts of a Judicial Opinion
1. Caption
2. Date of Decision
3. Docket Number
4. Headnotes/Syllabus
5. Names of Counsel and Judges
6. Opinion

Figure 5.5 Six Parts of a Judicial Opinion

1. **The Caption**—Also known as the style of the case; this is the names of the parties to the case. The caption also includes the legal citation. Think of the legal citation as address of the case. There are specific rules as to how to cite the name of the case found in *The Bluebook* and the *ALWD Citation Manual*.

2. **Date of decision**—the date on which the decision was handed down by the court.

3. **The docket number**—The docket number of the case represents the internal filing number of the court assigned by the clerk of court at the initiation associated with the matter. Every case has a docket number that corresponds to the alphanumeric number assigned to the case by the clerk of court at the beginning of the litigation. For search purposes the docket number is excellent at locating documents that are part of the case such as briefs, complaints, and other documents.

4. **The headnote and syllabus**—A headnote and a syllabus are considered research enhancements typically provided by a commercial publisher. Headnotes are usually written by editors employed by the publisher and sometimes the court. The editor reads the judicial opinion and extracts each point of law discussed in a case. An editor will summarize in their own words the decision of the court. The headnotes are not authority but rather a statement of the editor's view of the court's reasoning and decisions. Headnotes are based on language appearing in the actual opinion, but it is the language in the

Wells v. Liddy, 186 F.3d 505 (1999)

KeyCite Yellow Flag - Negative Treatment
Declined to Extend by Gilmore v. Jones, W.D.Va., March 29, 2019

1.Caption

186 F.3d 505
United States Court of Appeals,
Fourth Circuit.

Ida Maxwell WELLS, Plaintiff–Appellant,

v.

G. Gordon LIDDY, Defendant–Appellee,

3. Docket number Phillip Mackin Bailley, Movant.

No. 98–1962.

Argued March 3, 1999.

2. Date of decision Decided July 28, 1999.

Synopsis

Former secretary of Democratic National Committee (DNC) sued conspirator of Watergate burglary of DNC headquarters, alleging that he was defaming her by claiming she was involved in call-girl ring allegedly associated with DNC. The United States District Court for the District of Maryland, J. Frederick Motz, Judge, 1 F.Supp.2d 532, entered summary judgment for defendant, and plaintiff appealed. The Court of Appeals, Williams, Circuit Judge, held that: (1) under Maryland's choice-of-law rule, publication of speech given at university in Virginia occurred solely in Virginia; (2) speech on board ship on the high seas was governed by general maritime law; (3) it is predicted that Maryland would apply the law of plaintiff's domicile in cases of multistate broadcast defamation or publication from a world wide web site; (4) the university speech, the shipboard speech, and the web site statement were capable of defamatory meaning, but the radio statements were not; (5) defendant was not shown to be responsible for publication of the web site statement; (6) plaintiff was not a limited purpose public figure; (7) plaintiff was not an involuntary public figure; and (8) plaintiff raised a genuine issue of material fact on actual malice.

Reversed and remanded.

Procedural Posture(s): On Appeal; Motion for Summary Judgment.

4. Headnote

West Headnotes (58)

[1]   Federal Courts — Depositions and discovery
      Court of Appeals reviews the district court's management of the discovery process under the narrow abuse of discretion standard.

      7 Cases that cite this headnote

[2]   Federal Civil Procedure — Lack of cause of action or defense
      Summary judgment is appropriate when a party, who would bear the burden on the issue at trial, does not forecast evidence sufficient to establish an essential element of the case. Fed. Rules Civ.Proc.Rule 56(c), 28 U.S.C.A.

      7 Cases that cite this headnote

[3]   Federal Courts — Summary judgment
      Federal Courts — Summary judgment
      Court of Appeals reviews a grant of summary judgment de novo, viewing the facts in the light most favorable to the nonmoving party.

      1 Cases that cite this headnote

[4]   Federal Civil Procedure — Weight and sufficiency
      When the nonmoving party must produce clear and convincing evidence to support its claim, that higher evidentiary burden is considered as part of the summary judgment calculus.

      4 Cases that cite this headnote

[5]   Federal Courts — Constitutional rights, civil rights, and discrimination in general

WESTLAW © 2022 Thomson Reuters. No claim to original U.S. Government Works.

Figure 5.6 Parts of a Judicial Opinion Illustrated (A)

opinion that is controlling. Researchers may use the headnotes as a scanning tool to quickly evaluate whether it is worth spending further time with the decision or it is time to move on to the next source. On Westlaw and Lexis, headnotes are also excellent navigation tools that permit you to jump from the headnote to the place in the opinion where the point of law is discussed.

A syllabus may be prepared by the clerk of court, a judge, or a commercial publisher. The syllabus is not primary authority as it is a summary of the law and not the law, even when Justice

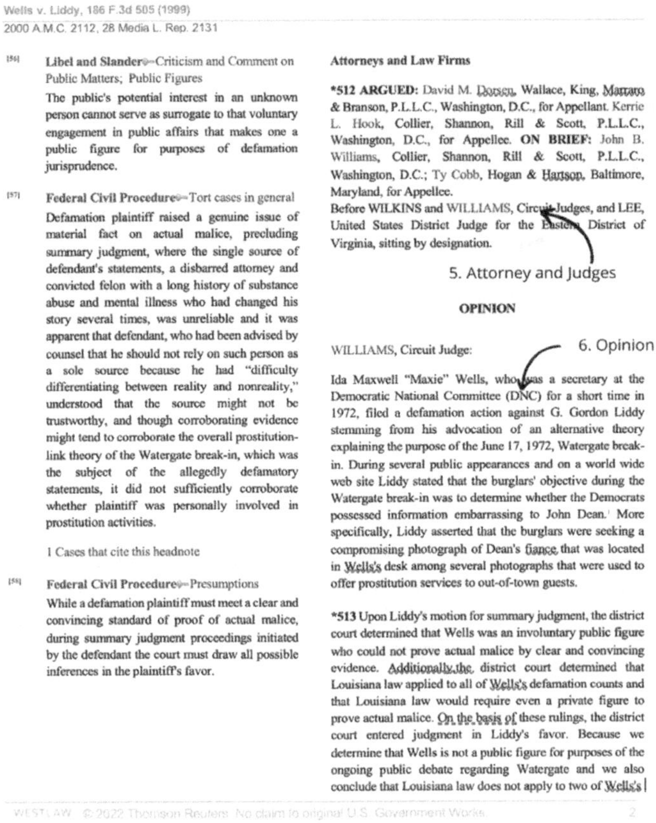

Wells v. Liddy, 186 F.3d 505 (1999)
2000 A.M.C. 2112, 28 Media L. Rep. 2131

[56] Libel and Slander—Criticism and Comment on Public Matters; Public Figures

The public's potential interest in an unknown person cannot serve as surrogate to that voluntary engagement in public affairs that makes one a public figure for purposes of defamation jurisprudence.

[57] Federal Civil Procedure—Tort cases in general

Defamation plaintiff raised a genuine issue of material fact on actual malice, precluding summary judgment, where the single source of defendant's statements, a disbarred attorney and convicted felon with a long history of substance abuse and mental illness who had changed his story several times, was unreliable and it was apparent that defendant, who had been advised by counsel that he should not rely on such person as a sole source because he had "difficulty differentiating between reality and nonreality," understood that the source might not be trustworthy, and though corroborating evidence might tend to corroborate the overall prostitution-link theory of the Watergate break-in, which was the subject of the allegedly defamatory statements, it did not sufficiently corroborate whether plaintiff was personally involved in prostitution activities.

1 Cases that cite this headnote

[58] Federal Civil Procedure—Presumptions

While a defamation plaintiff must meet a clear and convincing standard of proof of actual malice, during summary judgment proceedings initiated by the defendant the court must draw all possible inferences in the plaintiff's favor.

Attorneys and Law Firms

*512 ARGUED: David M. Dorsen, Wallace, King, Marram & Branson, P.L.L.C., Washington, D.C., for Appellant. Kerrie L. Hook, Collier, Shannon, Rill & Scott, P.L.L.C., Washington, D.C., for Appellee. ON BRIEF: John B. Williams, Collier, Shannon, Rill & Scott, P.L.L.C., Washington, D.C.; Ty Cobb, Hogan & Hartson, Baltimore, Maryland, for Appellee.

Before WILKINS and WILLIAMS, Circuit Judges, and LEE, United States District Judge for the Eastern District of Virginia, sitting by designation.

5. Attorney and Judges

OPINION

WILLIAMS, Circuit Judge: 6. Opinion

Ida Maxwell "Maxie" Wells, who was a secretary at the Democratic National Committee (DNC) for a short time in 1972, filed a defamation action against G. Gordon Liddy stemming from his advocacy of an alternative theory explaining the purpose of the June 17, 1972, Watergate break-in. During several public appearances and on a world wide web site Liddy stated that the burglars' objective during the Watergate break-in was to determine whether the Democrats possessed information embarrassing to John Dean.¹ More specifically, Liddy asserted that the burglars were seeking a compromising photograph of Dean's fiancé that was located in Wells's desk among several photographs that were used to offer prostitution services to out-of-town guests.

*513 Upon Liddy's motion for summary judgment, the district court determined that Wells was an involuntary public figure who could not prove actual malice by clear and convincing evidence. Additionally, the district court determined that Louisiana law applied to all of Wells's defamation counts and that Louisiana law would require even a private figure to prove actual malice. On the basis of these rulings, the district court entered judgment in Liddy's favor. Because we determine that Wells is not a public figure for purposes of the ongoing public debate regarding Watergate and we also conclude that Louisiana law does not apply to two of Wells's

Figure 5.6 Parts of a Judicial Opinion Illustrated (B)

Ginsburg has written her own syllabus. One helpful feature of the syllabus is the use of normalized language. In addition to serving as a quick scan for relevance to your research query, the syllabus also provides suggestions for search terms that may be useful in locating additional highly relevant sources.

As usual, there is an exception to this rule. The West Virginia Constitution requires the West Virginia Supreme Court to write and include an introductory set of notes called syllabus points that are to precede the text of the judicial opinion for every point of law in which a majority of the justices agree.[3]

---

3. W. VA. CONST. art. VIII, §4.

These points of law may be referred to by the West Virginia Supreme Court in subsequent opinions and are considered primary, binding authority in West Virginia.

5. **Counsel and judge names**—The opinion will include the names of counsel for the parties to the opinion and the judges hearing the matter. The name of the counsel and judge can be helpful in research by locating similar cases that a firm has litigated or a judge has decided. Judge and counsel names are search fields in Westlaw and Lexis.

6. **The opinion**—The opinion contains the primary authority in the holding of the case. It is this one specific part of the opinion that constitutes primary authority. Note it is only the holding in the majority opinion that constitutes the primary authority of the opinion. Obiter dictum or dicta is the expression of the judge of an opinion unessential to the decision.

Dicta Defined

An incidental expression of opinion not essential to the decision and not precedent.

Excerpted language from **Hays v. Sony Corp. of America, 847 F.2d 412 (7th Cir. 1988).**

The reasons for a presumption against finding academic writings to be work made for hire are as forceful today as they ever were. Nevertheless it is widely believed that the 1976 Act abolished the teacher exception, see Dreyfuss, *supra*, at 598–600; Simon, *supra*, at 502–09; *Weinstein v. University of Illinois,* 811 F.2d 1091, 1093–94 (7th Cir.1987)—though, if so, probably inadvertently, for there is no discussion of the issue in the legislative history, and no political or other reasons come to mind as to why Congress might have wanted to abolish the exception. To a literalist of statutory interpretation, the conclusion that the Act abolished the exception may seem inescapable. The argument would be that academic writing, being within the scope of academic employment, is work made for hire, per se; so, in the absence of an express written and signed waiver of the academic employer's rights, the copyright in such writing must belong to the employer. But considering the havoc that such a conclusion would wreak in the settled practices of academic institutions, the lack of fit between the policy of the work-for-hire doctrine and the conditions of academic production, and the absence of any indication that Congress meant to abolish the teacher exception, we might, if forced to decide the issue, conclude that the exception had survived the enactment of the [*417] 1976 Act. A possible textual handle may be found in the words of section 201(b), quoted earlier, which appear to require not only that the work be a work for hire but that it have been prepared *for* the employer—which the Hays–McDonald manual may or may not have been.

Figure 5.7 Dicta Example from Hays v. Sony Corp. of America, 847 F.2d 412 (7th Cir. 1988)

In *Hays v. Sony Corp. of America*, Judge Posner uses dicta to express personal views, his opinion, regarding the viability of teacher exception to copyright. While this may be words professors love to see in print, his statement is not essential to the determination of the case and qualifies as dicta. It is not precedent. Remember dicta is language that is not nec-essary to the decision of the court. Dicta can be hard to spot so consider these clues that the language may constitute dicta.

a. The court is discussing history of a legal concept.

b. Use of phraseology that indicates the discussion does not ad-dress the issue before the case.

c. Use of a hypothetical that discusses facts not actually before the court.

d. Look for clues the court is taking a sidebar or is on a tangent.

The essential point to remember is that dicta is never precedent. It may be persuasive but is never binding language.

Dicta

Think of dicta as an incidental or a passing remark. Consider the following as an example. Your study group is discussing the property concept of bailments. You offer up your chocolate chip recipe and offer to bake some for the next session of the study group. Another member of the study group prefers snickerdoo-dle cookies. While most may love the idea of chocolate chip cookies and while you may debate the virtues of chocolate chip versus snickerdoodle, the cookie debate has no bearing on the topic of bailments. The discussion of cookies is incidental to the issue and has no bearing on the discussion of bailments. **The cookie debate is dicta.**

Types of Judicial Opinions

The type of judicial opinion is important for the purposes of weight. The greatest weight is accorded to a majority opinion. It is the holding from the majority opinion that constitutes primary, binding authority or primary, persuasive authority. Courts, however, issue a variety of differ-ent types of opinions. The other commonly known opinion types are concurring and dissenting opinions. As a researcher you may wish to cite to a concurrence or dissent for purposes of persuasion; however, the language in a concurrence or dissent is never binding, it is only persua-

sive. Other common opinion types include plurality, per curiam, seria-
tim, and memorandum.

Types of Judicial Opinions, Generally	
Majority	An opinion joined in by more than half the judges considering a given case.
Concurring	An opinion by one or more judges who agree on the judgment reached but on different grounds from those expressed in the majority opinion.
Dissenting	An opinion by one or more judges who disagree with the decision reached by the majority.
Plurality	An opinion lacking enough judges' votes to constitute a majority, but receiving more votes than any other opinion.
Per curiam	An opinion handed down by an appellate court without identifying the individual judge who wrote the opinion.
Seriatim	A series of opinions written individually by each judge on the bench.
Memorandum	A unanimous opinion that succinctly states the decision of the court usually without elaboration because the decision follows a well-established legal principle.

Figure 5.8 Types of Judicial Opinions

On occasion, all judges of an intermediate court of appeals hear a
case. The term for this type of hearing is *en banc*. This takes place upon
successful petition to the court. Otherwise, the norm is for three judges
of an appellate court to hear and decide an appeal. En banc review is an
exception to the rule and traditionally reserved for complex matters or
matters in which the court decides there is an issue of significant importance. The Federal Rules of Appellate procedure disfavor en banc proceedings but such proceedings are permitted in unusual circumstances.[4]
Each circuit maintains their own rules regarding en banc proceedings.
A decision from an en banc panel carries significant weight as it is the
decision of all justices for that court rather than a subset of three justices.

To evaluate whether a judicial opinion may be cited as authority, you
must consider both the currency, or date of the decision, and its validity,
or if the decision remains good law. Judicial opinions are current as of
the date of the decision. Unlike other sources of law, the judicial opinion
is fixed as of that particular point in time. The law continues to accrete,

---

4. FED. R. APP. P. 35(a).

however. Because the law continues to grow and add to the corpus of the law, the citator is a valuable tool. Shepard's and KeyCite are the common examples of citators. The citator is a tool created to validate primary authority by evaluating its treatment in subsequent law, whether that be subsequent judicial opinions or legislation. A subsequent decision may question, criticize, or overrule an existing opinion. The legislature may enact a new law that overturns the decision in a case. Citators are discussed in detail in Chapters 14 and 18. In evaluating a judicial opinion for use it is important to note the currency or date of the decision and to validate that the decision remains good law.

Review What You've Read

1. You intend to assert that a specific case is strong precedent for your client's matter. In making such an assertion, what are you saying about each of the following?

   a. The holding of the case

   b. Jurisdiction

   c. Status as binding or persuasive precedent

2. Is the persuasive weight or value of an en banc decision greater than a decision from a three-judge panel?

3. What is a non-precedential or unpublished opinion and why is that meaningful to your research?

4. What are the steps of the publication process for a judicial opinion?

5. What are the parts of a judicial opinion?

6. What are the different types of judicial opinions?

Chapter 6

Statutes and Constitutions

Statutes

Characteristics of a Statute

1. Primary authority as created by the legislature in their law-making capacity.
2. Is binding authority within its controlling jurisdiction and neither persuasive nor binding outside the controlling jurisdiction.

A statute is a law passed by a legislature and signed by the executive that proscribes, directs, or prohibits a certain act. Statutes are published in a distinct three-step process. The names of the publications may vary among jurisdictions, but the steps remain the same.

Publication of a Statute

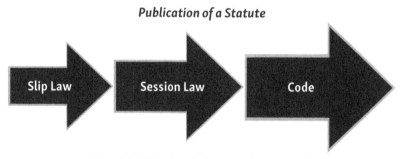

Figure 6.1 Publication of a Statute — Slip Law to Code

A statute is the final step in the creation of a law by the legislative branch. A statute is first published as a slip law. The slip law is the official text of the law in pamphlet format after it is passed by the legislature and signed by the executive. The slip law may also be published online on the legislature's website.

Slip Law Defined

The first publication of the law in pamphlet format. This publication contains the full text of the law, as passed by the legislature, and signed by the executive, and as identified by the public law number. The slip law will contain the chapter or law number.

Publication Process of Statutes—Public Law

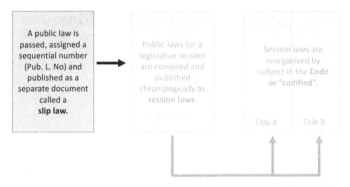

Figure 6.2 Publication Process of a Statute—Public Law 116-115

The construction of the public law number indicates the session of Congress that passed the law and the chronology of when the law was passed within that specific session of the legislature. For example, Public Law 116-115 indicates that it was passed by the 116th Congress session of the legislature and is the 115th law passed in such session.

Publication Process of Statutes—Session Laws

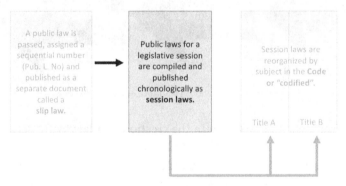

Figure 6.3 Publication Process of a Statute—Session Laws

Slip laws are then collected and published in chronological order in the session laws of the jurisdiction. At the federal level and at the end of a congressional session, all public and private slip laws are published in the *United States Statutes at Large*. The Statutes at Large is organized by session of Congress. At the state level, the session laws of the state legislature are similarly published in chronological order, but the name of the compilation may vary. For example, in Virginia the session laws are published as *Acts of Assembly*. In West Virginia the session laws are published as *Acts of the Legislature of West Virginia*. In North Carolina the session laws are published as the *Session Laws of North Carolina*. Table T1 of *The Bluebook* will assist you in identifying the appropriate nomenclature for your jurisdiction.

A citation to the Statutes at Large reads as follows: 134 Stat. 106. The first number, 134, is the volume of the Statutes at Large that contains the law. *Stat.* is the abbreviation for Statutes at Large, and the section number, 106, is the first page on which the law may be located. The law as it appears in the Statutes at Large will be identical to the text found in the slip law version. For research purposes, the session laws are the instance where a researcher finds the entire law as passed by the legislature.

Session Laws Defined

The permanent publication of slip laws enacted during a legislative session in chronological order. Publication occurs at the end of a legislative session.

The final or third step in the publication of a statute is the codification of the statute in a code. Codes are the subject matter classification of the law. As the session laws publish a statute in chronological order it is difficult to use the session law for research purposes. A legislative act may include laws that fall into multiple different topics. In the codification process, the new law is dissected based upon the subject matter classifications of the code and the subject matter of the legislation. Codification serves three purposes: (1) to reconcile the language of the original act with all amendments including additions or deletions of language; (2) a subject matter arrangement of all laws on a single topic in a single place; and (3) a version of the current laws in force eliminating repealed, superseded, and laws otherwise no longer in force.

In the codification process the original text of the statute is preserved intact as it appeared in the slip law, but the provisions are rearranged or grouped based on the fixed subject matter categories. This permits the researcher to find the statutes relating to one topic in a single place in logical order as opposed to scattered among the various session laws. For example, if you want to see the original substance of the Patriot Act as it was passed by Congress, you will want to use the Statutes at Large. The Patriot Act as originally passed is a large group of additions and amendments to existing statutes throughout the U.S. Code. If I want to know everywhere substance was added, deleted, or otherwise changed, it is best to look at the act as passed in the Statutes at Large rather than individual code sections. Codification permits indexing the new law based upon the topics included in the law. For example, searching by subject matter for copyright, codified within Title 17 of the United States Code, is infinitely easier than thumbing through pages of new laws in chronological order. This is why we use codes to locate relevant statutes rather than session laws. The other benefit is the incorporation of amendments and deletion of repealed laws to create a logical and current statement of our law.

This begs the question of why does a researcher care about session laws? There are three specific reasons: (1) The session law is the most authoritative form of the law. Session laws control when there is a discrepancy in the wording of the law between the code and the session law. (2) Conducting legislative history research, specifically in determining when and how the law the text of the law has changed over time. (3) Conducting historical research, for example to determine what the law was at a specific point in time in the past.

Codes publish only the public laws that constitute the general and permanent statutes of a specific jurisdiction based on a fixed topic or subject matter arrangement.

Federal Acts

*Each new act passed by Congress is either a
public law or a private law*

Public Laws—an act passed by the legislature with permanent general application to the public at large.

Private Laws—an act passed by the legislature for the specific benefit of an individual or a small group. The most common use of a private law is in the instance of immigration granting citizenship. Private laws are not codified and appear exclusively in the session laws.

Publication Process of Statutes—Code

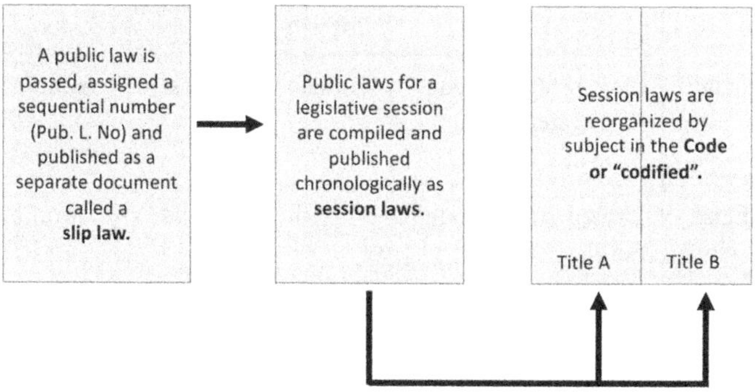

Figure 6.4 Publication Process of a Statute—Code

Codes are generally organized by topic, with each topic subdivided into smaller granular topics. For example, the federal code is organized into fifty-four titles: each title represents a distinct subject matter or area of the law. For example, Title 17 of the United State Code contains the laws of copyright. Titles are then subdivided into chapters and finally into sections. State codes are more varied. They may follow the same organizational principles as the federal code, or they may elect a different structure. For example, Texas has distinct codes based on subject, like the Property Code, Estates Code, and Family Code and Virginia organizes its code based on sections rather than titles.[1]

As with judicial opinions, a code may be designated as official or unofficial. The designation of official will attach if the government authority arranges for the publication of the code. A commercial publisher that is designated as the publisher of the code by the government publishes

---

1. Texas Constitution and Statutes at https://statutes.capitol.texas.gov (last visited April 4, 2022).

the official code. Jurisdictions may have official and unofficial codes if there are multiple codes published. At the federal level there are three versions of the code, two unofficial and one official.

Codes Containing Statutes of the United States			
Official	United States Code—U.S.C.	Published by the Government Publishing Office	Unannotated
Unofficial	United States Code Annotated—U.S.C.A.	Published by West	Annotated
Unofficial	United States Code Service—U.S.C.S.	Published by Lexis	Annotated

Figure 6.5 Codes Containing Statutes of the United States

The annotated code is the preferred source for research due to the editorial content and *value-added research tools* included by commercial publishers in addition to the text of the statute. An annotated code may be an official or unofficial code. Most annotated codes are commercially published. An annotation includes case summaries and citations to secondary sources that explain or comment on the law. The annotation provides a cite or refence to the case that discusses the statute. It is a quick way of identifying a case that discusses the operation of the statute and is valuable in interpreting and applying the language of the statute. These value-added materials, like the annotations, are tools that assist the researcher in understanding the language of the law and applying the law. The text and arrangement of the law in an annotated and unannotated version of the law or an official or unofficial code will be the same. The annotated code is a fully integrated research tool combining the law, or primary source, with explanatory materials, secondary sources that make research quick and easy. While the text of the law is the same regardless of the choice of code, there are distinctions among commercial codes. For example, the U.S.C.A. published by West contains more comprehensive annotations when compared to the selective approach adopted by the U.S.C.S. published by Lexis. It is a matter of quantity over quality.

Annotated Code	
Value-Added Material by Type	Description of contents.
Historical Note	Information detailing the history of the statute, including date of original enactment, dates of amendments and legislative history.
Cross-Reference	Citations to regulations and secondary sources.
Research References	Information on related topics, references to secondary sources providing explanatory material, references to regulatory provisions implementing the statute.
Annotations/ Notes of Decision	Summaries of cases interpreting the law, often arranged by subject. This abstract created by an editor is a description that permits browsing by the researcher to locate relevant cases.

Figure 6.6 Features of the Annotated Code

Codes are periodically updated to contain the current law. The update schedule will vary based upon the code. Researchers using an online research platform like Westlaw or Lexis will note the frequent updates to include new material—amendments, repeals, and new laws. Updates may be as quick as two business days for federal materials and as long as a month or more for state law materials. As the update schedule varies widely, it is always important to check the update schedule and currency of the provision. Currency of a federal statute in an online database is as of a specific public law. The currency should not be confused with the effective date of the statute. The effective date of the statute is the date set by the legislature for the act take effect, becoming legally binding, operable, and enforceable. This may be as of a specific date or as of the end of a legislative session. Currency of a statute references when it was most recently updated to include the most recent amendments or other revisions. Currency of a state statute is frequently as of the conclusion of a specific legislative session.

Model acts also known as model laws are exactly that—a model for suggested language. Two of the best-known model laws are the Uniform Probate Code and the Uniform Commercial Code. The Uniform Law Commission and the American Bar Association are two organizations responsible for drafting and compiling the text of model laws. Model laws may be adopted by a legislature verbatim or a legislature may adopt the proposed text of the legislation with modifications. The *Uniform Laws Annotated* contains the text of all uniform laws recommended for adoption by a jurisdiction. Also known as the U.L.A., the set is available in print in most law libraries and on Westlaw. The term *model law* is a misnomer as they are suggestions, not law. Thus the U.L.A. is a secondary source and persuasive, not binding. If your jurisdiction has enacted a version of the model law, the binding, primary authority version of the law will be found in the jurisdiction's code. For example, if I wish to find the West Virginia UCC provision on *purchase money security interests,* the source I want is the West Virginia Code, not the U.L.A. In this instance, the West Virginia Code is the primary, binding authority and the U.L.A. merely a secondary source.

Look to a statute when:

1. You believe the law originated with a legislature.
2. You believe the case law was modified by the legislature to overturn or modify present case law.
3. When in doubt as statutes cover most areas of law.

Constitutions

A constitution documents the boundaries or frame of a political entity's system of laws. It is a description of the rules by which the entity operates. The frame permits the allocation of power and associated responsibilities among the designated branches of government. Some constitutions also define the basic rights bestowed to the individual. A constitution may be brief or extensive, written or unwritten, or uncodified.

The United States Constitution states:

> *This Constitution, and the laws of the United States which shall be made in pursuance thereof; and all treaties made, or which shall be made, under the authority of the United States, shall be the supreme law of the land; and the judges in every state shall be bound thereby, anything in the Constitution or laws of any State to the contrary notwithstanding.*[2]

---

2. U.S. Const. art. VI, cl 2.

Authority for acts, joint resolutions, treaties, and interstate compacts—all types of federal legislation—is provided by the Constitution. The text of the Constitution may be found in numerous sources, including *Blacks' Law Dictionary*, each instance of the federal code, state codes, and online. Similarly, the text of a state constitution may be found in the state's code.

Resources for Constitutional Law Research	
Sources for Federal Constitutional Research	*Sources for State Constitutional Research*
United States Code Annotated	State Code for the jurisdiction
United States Code Service	Constitutions of the United States: National and State
The Constitution of the United States of America	State Constitutional Conventions, Commissions, and Amendments
Encyclopedia of the American Constitution	Sources and Documents of United States Constitutions
The Founders' Constitution	Index Digest of State Constitutions
Constitutional Amendments, 1789 to date	
Comprehensive Bibliography of the American Connotational and Legal History	
The Constitution of the United States: A Guide and Bibliography to Current Scholarly Research	
American Constitutional Law	
Treatise on Constitutional Law: Substance and Procedure	
Modern Constitutional Law	
Documents Illustrative of the Formation of the Union of American States	

Table continues on next page

Table continued from last page

Resources for Constitutional Law Research	
Sources for Federal Constitutional Research	*Sources for State Constitutional Research*
Documentary History of the Constitution of the United States of America, 1786–1870	
The Federalist	

Figure 6.7 Resources for Constitutional Law Research

Researching issues of constitutional law usually involves more than simply finding the text of the constitutional provision. A researcher is likely to need to locate interpretative and explanatory material on the topic in addition to the universe of case law interpreting the provision. An annotated text of the Constitution includes the value-added research references helpful in statutory research. An annotated code is often the best research option for locating an annotated version of a constitution.

Federal Legislative History

School House Rock: I'm Just a Bill

I'm just a bill. Yes, I'm only a bill. And I'm sitting here on Capitol Hill. Well, it's a long, long journey to the Capital City. It's a long, long wait while I'm sitting in committee. But I know some day, at least I hope and pray that I will, but today I'm still a bill....[3]

A discussion of statutes would be incomplete without discussion of what comes before. The statute is the product of the conclusion of the legislative law-making process. What comes before is a complicated process resulting in the enacted law. This chapter focuses on the process of federal legislation. For most states, the process of creating a statute is similar; however, conducting a legislative history at the state level varies widely and depends upon the specific state. If you need to compile a

---

3. American Rock, *I'm Just a Bill* (School House Rock and ABC 1976).

legislative history of a state law, this is time to phone a friend—your friendly law librarian.

The federal legislative process is a long and winding process. Understanding the process itself is helpful to account for the documents created along the way. It is imperative to recall that the only primary authority in the legislative process is the final product, the law, the statute. Everything that comes before is considered persuasive authority, so all documents in a legislative history are merely persuasive. Researchers use the term *legislative history* to refer to the documents created as part of the legislative process. Investigating the documentary history of a law will assist you in understanding the legislative intent.

Legislative History and Legislative Intent Defined

Legislative history—*(1) the documentary history of the legislative process creating a law; (2) a reference to the documents that contain the information considered by the legislature prior to enacting a law.*

Legislative intent—*the intent of the legislative body as a whole.*

Compiling a legislative history is a lengthy and time-intensive process and one not undertaken lightly. Researching legislative histories is addressed comprehensively in Chapter 22 of this text but is introduced here to give important context to our discussion of statutes. The threshold requirement for conducting a legislative history is the presence of an ***unresolved ambiguity*** in the statute. The qualifier *unresolved* is significant. If there is a statutory ambiguity but a court has since resolved the ambiguity by a binding judicial opinion, then the ambiguity is now resolved, and legislative history research is no longer necessary. Other situations in which a legislative history may be helpful are: (1) application of the statute in an unforeseen situation and (2) suggestion of a new or different interpretation of the statute.

Steps in Compiling a Legislative History

1. Presence of an unresolved ambiguity
2. Determination of the presence or absence of compiled legislative history
3. Identification of the documents in the legislative process.

The documents produced as part of the legislative process cannot be viewed out of context of that process. By definition, these documents are persuasive, but the weight or persuasive value will vary by context. The documents created throughout the legislative process contain the expressions of members of Congress and others as evidence of the intent of a legislature at that point in time. Documents that contain the expressions of a member of Congress generally carry more persuasive value than ancillary documents that contain the expressions of others, but are considered by the legislators. Any document considered in the legislative process may be of assistance in identifying legislative intent. The other thing to remember is that not every bill goes through every part of the legislative process.

How a Bill Becomes a Law

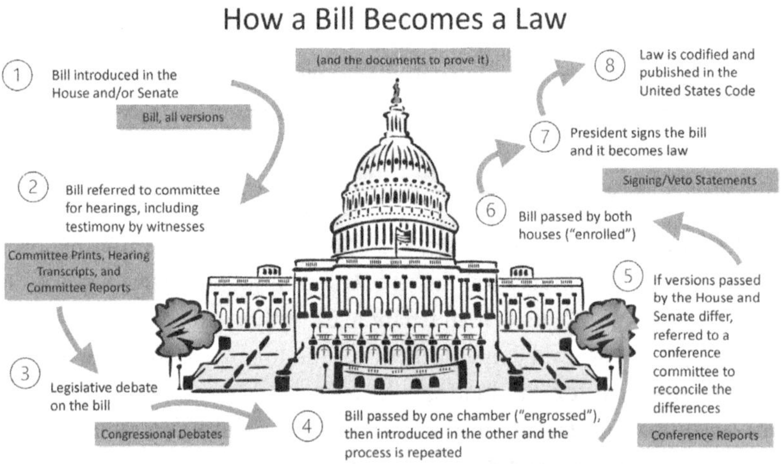

Figure 6.8 The Legislative Process and Documents

Step 1: Introduction of the Bill

The Bill Number
H.R. 455, 106th Cong. or S. 1, 106th Cong.

- *H.R. or S. will be assigned based on the chamber of the legislature.*
- *The number of the bill representing its place in the line of proposed bills for a specific session of Congress.*
- *At the end of a session, any bill not enacted as law dies and must start the process over with a reintroduction and a new number.*

The bill[4] is a legislative proposal and is the first legislative document. A piece of legislation begins the legislative process when introduced by a member of Congress.[5] The member places the bill in the *hopper*. At that point the bill is assigned a bill number indicating the session of Congress and the chronological order of the introduction of the bill in the legislative session. The bill is then assigned to a committee. The text of the bill may be amended at any point in the process. This makes the bill variations meaningful as comparisons of the text will highlight the addition and deletion of text. These changes are indicative of meaning and intent.

Step 2: The Congressional Hearing—The Transcript

Hearings are held pursuant to the committee structure of Congress. They investigate, explore, and generate views of people interested in legislative action. Hearings can occur out of the traditional sequence of the legislative process. They can occur prior to the introduction of the bill and over multiple sessions of the legislature. The purpose of the hearing is to provide information on the topic for use of members of Congress in the consideration of proposed legislation. As a hearing does not reflect congressional deliberation, technically it is not part of a legislative history and reflects the statements and views of non-legislators. However, the transcript of a hearing may be useful in: (1) determining why certain language is included or deleted from a bill, (2) noting the testimony of members of Congress as part of the hearing process, and (3) noting the information members of Congress considered during the legislative process.

The document produced from the hearing is a transcript. Transcripts of a hearing may be published or unpublished, open or closed, and *published but unpublished.*[6] In terms of the authority of the hearing as evidence of legislative intent, it is one of the least persuasive documents of a legislative history, ranking below the committee report and the bill.

_____

4. A joint resolution may also be introduced as the proposed law. There is no substantial distinction between a bill and a joint resolution.

5. The House of Representatives and the Senate are collectively referred to as Congress. Congress meets in a two-year period known as a session.

6. Some hearings are designated as unpublished but have been published by a commercial service making them unpublished but published.

The low persuasive value assigned is due to the presence of bias in addition to the fact that it is typically a person, not a legislator, providing comment and testimony. Testimony in a hearing is likely to include a range of persons from the partisan to the disinterested expert. Use of hearing testimony as evidence of legislative intent requires discrimination by the user.

Step 3: The Committee — The Committee Report

The committee produces the most valuable and most persuasive document of a legislative history, the committee report. This document reflects the outcome of the process of those most closely associated with the current text of the legislation. The committee report accompanies the bill reported out of committee to the floor of either the House or Senate for debate. The committee report is considered the most valuable indicia of legislative intent as it represents the consensus of the committee and is the one document containing a systematic affirmation of legislative intent. The report contains a section-by-section analysis reflecting the recommended text of the law along with the Committee's analysis of the content and stated intent. The committee's rational supporting recommendation and, occasionally, a minority statement stating the rationale for any disagreement, may also be included. Almost every bill reported out of committee will have a committee report.

The conference report is the report of a conference committee. The conference committee is the committee appointed to reconcile different versions of a law passed by the House and the Senate. Such committee will have members from both legislative chambers. The conference committee reconciles the differences into a compromise and sends the compromised bill back to each chamber for passage. The committee report from the conference committee will contain the text of the compromise bill. The report of the conference committee is highly persuasive.

The Committee Print is a document created or used by a congressional committee on a topic related to legislation or research. They typically include historical or statistical information used in analysis of legislation. Content of committee prints may include draft reports, directories, statistics, investigative reports, historical reports, situational studies hearings, and legislative analysis. A committee print is usually background information with no or limited public distribution. They have limited persuasive value on the topic of legislative intent.

Step 4: Congressional Debates—The Floor Proceedings

Once a bill is reported out of committee it is sent to the floor of the House or Senate for consideration and debate, although floor debate may occur at any point in the process. Arguments for and against passage are made, amendments may be offered and passed or defeated, and explanations of language offered. This conversation is documented through recording in the Congressional Record. There are two versions of the Congressional Record—the daily version, which is published first, and the permanent edition. The record of debate is preserved almost verbatim in the Congressional Record. We say *almost* verbatim because legislators have the right to edit their remarks. The Congressional Record is published each day of a session of Congress.

The remarks of legislators made on the floor of a chamber during debate might suggest a high indication of legislative intent and a corresponding high degree of persuasive value. The opposite is true. Many legislators do not participate in the floor debate. Others submit remarks to the record post-debate, others edit their remarks, and still others provide remarks even when they did not participate. This means that the record is not actually a transcript of what is said on the floor of a chamber during debate. As a rule of thumb, the remarks of the bill sponsor tend to be the most valuable as they are responsible for shepherding the bill through debate to passage. Use of the permanent edition of the Congressional Record is preferred for citation purposes per the citation manuals. The Congressional Record—Daily Edition is more readily available in online research platforms and databases. It is important to note the distinction between the permanent and daily editions as the pagination is distinct between the two versions.

Step 5: The Executive—Presidential Signing Statements and the Veto

A bill passed by both chambers becomes an enrolled bill. The enrolled bill is sent to the President for signature, making it law or veto.

Definition

Engrossed bill—*a bill passed by one but not both chambers of the legislature*

Enrolled bill—*a bill passed by both chambers and presented for approval (signature) to the President.*

The President has two options. The first is to approve or sign the bill into law, creating a new law. The second is to veto the legislation. If the President vetoes a bill, it is returned to Congress. At that point both the House and Senate must approve passage of the bill by a two-thirds majority for the bill to become law. A President may elect to document his intent as to signature or veto with a message or statement. The message usually takes the form of a Presidential Signing or Veto Statement. This statement can provide information on legislative or, at least, executive intent. The statement may be found in any of several places. *The Daily Compilation of Presidential Documents*[7] and *United States Code Congressional and Administrative News* are the two most frequently used sources.

Review What You've Read

1. What is the distinction between the *United States Code* and the *United States Statutes at Large*?

2. When a government arranges for the publication of a code, what designation do we assign to such code?

3. What information may be found in an annotated code?

4. What documents may be found in a legislative history?

5. What is the threshold requirement for compiling a legislative history?

---

7. Note, prior to the Obama White House, this was known as The Weekly Compilation of Presidential Documents.

Chapter 7

Rules and Regulations

Characteristics of Rules and Regulations

1. Primary authority.
2. Code of Federal Regulations and Federal Register are the official sources for federal rules or regulations.
3. Properly promulgated rule has the force and effect of a statute.
4. Regulations are created by an agency pursuant to the delegation of authority from the legislative branch.

The modern administrative state is largely a product of the growth of the administrative agency in the early 1900s and particularly responding to the legislation of Franklin Roosevelt's New Deal. The administrative agency exists at both the federal and state levels.

Alphabet Soup

Agencies exist under a variety of names. Federal Bureau of Investigation (FBI), Federal Communications Commission (FCC), Food and Drug Administration (FDA). They are typically referred to by their initials rather than their name.

An agency is created by an act of the legislative branch but is part of the executive branch. Consider the presence of administrative authority in fifteen cabinet departments (State, Interior, Homeland Security, as examples), independent agencies (EPA, FCC, CIA, NRC, Federal Reserve Board), government organizations and corporations (USPS, FDIC, TVA, AMTRAK) estimated at over 400 departments, agencies, and sub-agencies. The agency is tasked with the enforcement and implementation of legislation. An agency receives a specific delegation of authority from the legislative branch to the executive branch. This delegation of derivative authority is referred to as *enabling legislation*. If you are researching an administrative law question, you should always understand the underlying legislation that authorized the agency providing the derivative authority for its rule-making capacity. The enabling act creates the frame or scope of the authority of the agency. In the final rule an authority note appears. This note is a cross-reference to the enabling legislation providing the authority for the agency to engage in this specific rulemaking.

For example, as a researcher you are interested in the regulations regarding eligibility requirements for the Rural Housing Site Loan Policies. You identify 7 C.F.R. §1822.265 Loan Purposes as relevant to your question. You note 42 U.S.C. §1480 as the enabling legislation using the authority note found at the end of the regulation.

> (42 U.S.C. 1480; delegation of authority by the Sec. of Agri., 7 CFR 2.23; delegation of authority by the Asst. Sec. for Rural Development, 7 CFR 2.70)

Figure 7.1 Example of Authority Note

An agency may only act within the boundaries of the scope of the enabling legislation. What an agency may do is dictated by the enabling language. Agencies perform various tasks as part of their mission. Those tasks include promulgation of regulations and adjudication of a controversy as set forth by the terms of the enabling statute.

Similarly, the limits of these tasks are set by the scope of authority designated in the enabling statute. At no time may an agency exceed the limit of authority delegated to it by the legislature. For example, in 2011, the IRS issued regulations governing the activities of paid tax-return preparers (requiring exams and continuing education).[1] Three of those tax-return preparers sued, contending that the IRS exceeded its authority under the relevant statutes. The federal courts agreed with the paid tax-return preparers.[2]

---

1. 31 C.F.R. §230 (2010).
2. Loving v. I.R.S., 920 F. Supp. 2d 108 (2013).

Permissible Agency Actions	
Rules or Regulations	Statements of general application by an agency to implement, interpret, or describe law or policy; properly promulgated such rule or regulation carries the same legal effect as a statute
Orders	The final disposition of an agency matter
Licenses	Permission, generally in the form of a permit or certificate
Advisory Opinions	Advice regarding contemplated action; authoritative interpretation of a statute or regulation
Decisions	End of an adjudicative matter

Figure 7.2 Permissible Agency Actions[3]

Often the language of the statute passed by the legislature lacks specificity or has gaps as the legislators do not have sufficient expertise of the topic to draft the required language. In these instances, it is common for the legislature to leave to the agency the job of filling the gap with the detail necessary for the enforcement of the act. For example, the migratory bird law is part of the Clean Water Act. The text of the Clean Water Act references migratory birds but fails to define what a migratory bird is. This leaves a gap in enforcement. The EPA, charged with enforcing the Clean Water Act, needs to know what qualifies as a migratory bird. As part of the enabling statute, Congress delegated authority to the EPA to fill the gap and tell everyone what qualifies as a migratory bird. The agency, circumscribed by the delegation of authority by the enabling statute, will fill in the detail or technical knowledge needed to permit the legislation to be enforced. Agencies create the detail through the promulgation of a rule or regulation. The terms *rule* and *regulation* are used interchangeably. The rule will appear like a statute, but the rule is a derivative of the enabling statute. Despite being derivative of the enabling statute, regulations are a source of law and accordingly constitute binding, primary authority.

---

3. The scope of the permissible action of an agency is dependent upon the delegation of authority found in the enabling statute documenting the delegation of authority from the legislative branch to the executive. ROY M. MERSKY AND DONALD J. DUNN, FUNDAMENTALS OF LEGAL RESEARCH (8th ed. 2002).

The Administrative Procedure Act sets out the requirements for promulgation of a rule.[4] They are:

1. Public notice of intent to regulate on a topic (i.e., create a rule).
2. Publication of the proposed language of the rule.
3. Public comment period.
4. Publication of the final rule of general applicability and legal effect prior to the effective date to place the public on notice of the rule.

There are two publications that contain the federal rules of *general applicability and legal effect.*

> A document of *general applicability and legal effect* is one issued under proper authority prescribing a right, privilege, authority, immunity, or imposing an obligation applicable to the general public members of a specifically defined class or group. Distinguished from a document that applies to a named individual, specific group, or organization[5]

The *Code of Federal Regulations,* also known as the C.F.R., and the *Federal Register* contain regulations of general applicability and legal effect. The Federal Register is published each business day excluding Federal holidays. This publication publishes rules in chronological order by agency and contains much more information than the C.F.R. Information appearing in the Federal Register is required to be accorded judicial notice.[6] It is also the first place a rule will appear in published format. A properly promulgated rule must first appear in the Federal Register as it is the source for all generally applicable rules. It is required by statute[7] to publish presidential proclamations, Executive Orders with general applicability and legal effect, documents that the President determines have general applicability and legal effect, proposed rules,

---

4. Administrative Procedure Act, 5 U.S.C. §§551–559 (2022).

5. FUNDAMENTALS OF LEGAL RESEARCH at 260.

6. Pub. L. No. 96-354. 94 Stat. 1164 (1980) (codified as amended at 5 U.S.C. §§601–612 (2000)).

7. Federal Register Act, 49 Stat 500 (1935).

temporary rules, final rules, regulatory agenda, notice of hearing, and notices generally.

Proposed rules are mere proposals. Think of them as the equivalent of the bill in the legislative process. It is the introduction of regulatory proposal and the initiation of the process to create a regulation. The rulemaking process begins with statutory authorization granting the agency the power to make a rule. The relevant agency then proposes the language of the proposed rule publishing it in the Federal Regulation. To have a properly promulgated regulation, proposed rules must be published in the Federal Register. The Notice of Proposed Rulemaking must:

1. identify the statute authorizing the rule
2. print the text and structure of the proposed rule
3. state why the rule is proposed
4. include a summary of the rule and related dates
5. include contact information for public comment
6. include supplementary information, including data relied upon, merits of the proposed rule, choices, and reasoning

The comment period for a proposed rule is usually thirty to sixty days but can be as long as one hundred eighty for complex regulations. Proposed rules currently available for comment can be found at www.regulations.gov in the view docket folder, comments.

At the conclusion of the comment period, the agency will consider the comments, revise the rule as appropriate, and issue a final rule. The final rule will be published in the Federal Register and then later codified as part of the C.F.R. It can also be found at https://regulations.gov.

Temporary regulations have the force of law like a final regulation, where proposed regulations do not. A temporary regulation has immediate effect upon publication in the Federal Register but expires at the end of three years except regulations issued prior to 1989.[8] They are issued to provide immediate guidance and may be relied upon.

The C.F.R. is a code that contains final rules. In other words, it is a subject matter arrangement of the regulations in force. It is updated on a

---

8. 26 U.S.C. §7805(e) (2022).

rolling quarterly basis. The C.F.R. has fifty titles like the arrangement of the United States Code. While both are arranged by title, the subject matter of the titles is different. For example, title 26 of the U.S.C. is the topic for the Internal Revenue Service. The I.R.S. regulations are found in title 20 of the C.F.R. Titles of the C.F.R. are divided into chapters that contain regulations of a specific agency within that topic. Chapters may be further divided into subchapters, then parts, and finally sections. Currency of a final rule is as of a specific volume and page of the *Federal Register*.

The C.F.R. provision, in addition to having an authority note that refers the researcher to the place in the U.S.C. where the text of the enabling legislation appears, also includes a *source note*. Using our example of regulations regarding eligibility requirements for the Rural Housing Site Loan Policies, you identified 7 C.F.R. §1822.265 Loan Purposes as relevant to your question. You note 35 FR 1607, July 1, 1970, as the place the final rule originally appeared in the Federal Register. You also note the rule was amended in 1978 and 2015 and the references to the places in the Federal Register where the language of the amendments may be found. This is the source note.

> [35 FR 16087, July 1, 1970, as amended at 43 FR 24264, June 5, 1978; 80 FR 9866, Feb. 24, 2015]

Figure 7.3 Example of Source Note

The source note is the reference to the place in the Federal Register where the language of the final rule appears. In addition to the text of the final rule as of its effective date, the final rule will usually include a preamble. The preamble to the final rule contains helpful information including a summary, effective date, and supplementary information. The preamble is a mini regulatory history of the rule, including a rationale as to why the rule is necessary. The preamble includes helpful information such as:

- the basis and purpose of the rule,
- facts and data an agency relied on in the creation of the rule,
- a response to comments and criticisms from the notice and comment function of the rulemaking process, and
- the goal or problem the rule is intended to address.

Publication Process of Regulations

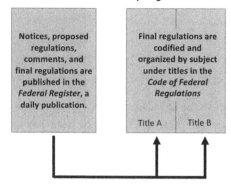

Figure 7.4 Publication Process of Regulations

Remember

Only the final rule appears in the C.F.R. The Federal Register is often the only source for other information published there.

Statutes to Regulations Comparison
C.F.R. is to U.S. Code as Federal Register is to Statutes at Large

Figure 7.5 Statutes to Regulations Comparison

Comparison of Federal Register and Code of Federal Regulations	
Federal Register	*Code of Federal Regulations (C.F.R.)*
Daily publication	Annual—updated yearly in quarters
New volume at the start of each year consecutively paginated	Fifty titles subdivided into chapters, parts, sections and organized by subject
Includes proposed rules, temporary rules, final rules, notices, Presidential documents, preamble to the final rule, and Unified Agenda	Final rules

Figure 7.6 Comparison of Federal Register and Code of Federal Regulations

Look for regulatory authority when:

1. The problem involves an administrative agency.
2. The law tends to be highly technical and detailed.
3. The area of law is highly regulated such as tax, environmental law, or securities law.

Once you identify and locate a relevant regulation, review the table of contents for the chapter, subchapter, or part. Identify the sections in the applicable unit and note the authority of the enabling legislation or statute.

Review What You've Read

1. What is a regulation? Name three types of regulations and why they are distinct.

2. What type of information will you locate in the *Code of Federal Regulations*?

3. What type of information will you locate in the *Federal Register*?

Summary—Primary Authority

Review of Publication Process

Publication Process Comparison

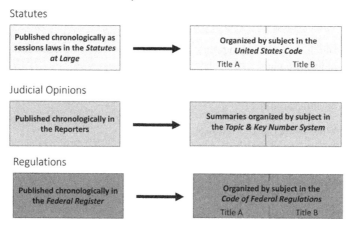

Figure 7.7 Publication Process of Primary Authorities

Review What You've Read Part II—
Primary Authority

1. Describe the concept and significance of weight in your own words.

2. What is dicta?

3. Detail the publication process for each of the following: statute, judicial opinion, and regulation.

4. When would you use the Statutes at Large as a research source over an annotated code?

5. What is the role of a citator?

6. What is the most persuasive document in a legislative history?

SECONDARY AUTHORITY SOURCES

Secondary sources are materials that comment on, explain, or assist the researcher in finding the law. Everything that is not a constitution, statute, rule, or judicial opinion is considered secondary authority. Secondary sources are, at best, persuasive, and some secondary sources, such as Restatements and treatises, are more persuasive than others, like A.L.R. annotations and legal encyclopedia entries.

> *Sources that fall into the category of secondary sources are never binding authority. At best they are persuasive, and not all secondary authority sources are even persuasive.*

Think back to the decision tree for authority. The second question in the decision tree is to determine if the source is primary or secondary. If you determine the source is secondary, you know the authority of the source is persuasive, but you should take your evaluation to the next step.

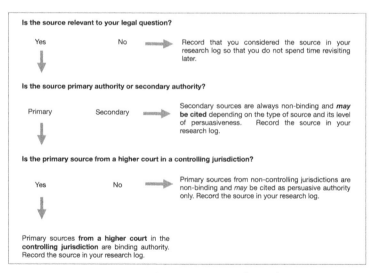

Figure 7.8 Authority Decision Tree (Repeat)

Understanding when not to use a secondary resource is also important. Do not use a secondary source as the exclusive basis of legal argument. Do use a secondary source to educate yourself about a specific area of law. Secondary sources have a purpose beyond citation. Understanding an area of law, the legal jargon used in that area, and how the law is applied is important and often best grasped with some introductory reading to create a baseline understanding.

The universe of secondary sources is broad and, when effectively used, adds value or relevance to the research process. Consider the analogy of a doctor with the option of different drugs to treat a malady. Understanding the side effects and selecting the best drug for the unique patient is their job. As a lawyer, it is your job to understand the different types of secondary sources, the unique characteristics of a source, and when to use a specific source. There are five secondary sources commonly used by researchers: the legal encyclopedia, *Restatements of Law*, treatises, legal periodicals, and *American Law Reports*. In addition to these five, you will also see the legal dictionary, *Words and Phrases Judicially Defined*, and hornbooks.

How do I select a secondary source? The array of secondary sources is broad and not every secondary source is appropriate for every research query.

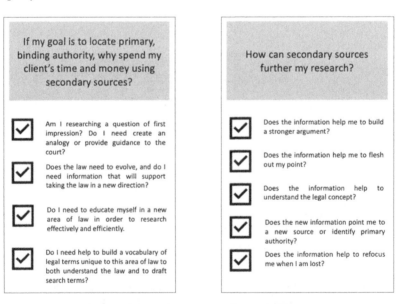

Figure 7.9 Secondary Source Evaluation—Criteria

Consider your purpose. What is it you need to find? Is it background information, primary authority, additional support for your argument, education on a topic? What level or depth of discussion would best satisfy my research needs? If a brief overview is best, I may choose a source like an A.L.R. annotation or legal encyclopedia entry. If a thorough and comprehensive discussion is needed, then a treatise is a better choice. Is my jurisdiction national or state specific? What is the source's audience? Is the audience of the publication meant to be law students, practitioners, or academics? Is the source current?

Chapter 8

The Legal Encyclopedia

Characteristics of the Legal Encyclopedia

1. General overview of the law by subject matter.
2. Used to educate the researcher on an area of law.
3. Identifies legal vocabulary unique to the area of law.
4. Provides background information.
5. Provides citations to primary authority.
6. Not appropriate for citation to a court.[1]
7. Written in narrative form.

Encyclopedias are sets of books that contain a broad number of topics arranged in alphabetical order, with a general discussion of each topic but lacking analysis and development. The legal encyclopedia is similar in structure to a general knowledge encyclopedia with the topics limited to law. A phrase to help remember the nature of an encyclopedia is *breadth but not depth.* The discussion is that of an introduction of the state of the law lacking in analysis or development of the law. The legal encyclopedia is an excellent starting point to educate the researcher, assist in identification of legal vocabulary unique to the area, and provide cross-references to other authorities in the area.

At the national level there are two legal encyclopedias, *American Jurisprudence, Second Edition,*[2] known as Am Jur., and *Corpus Juris Secundum,* known as C.J.S.[3]

---

1. *See* Chapter 13, footnote 1 herein regarding the citation to legal encyclopedia.
2. American Jurisprudence Second Edition is preceded by American Jurisprudence First Edition.
3. Corpus Juris Secundum is preceded by Corpus Juris.

Figure 8.1 Corpus Juris Secundum and American Jurisprudence 2d

Both are general legal encyclopedias that contain a survey of topics of law and are national in scope. These legal encyclopedias cover more than 400 discrete topics arranged in alphabetical order, making it likely that your topic is covered. Information is well indexed and easily discovered using the index or table of contents. Am Jur. is available on both Westlaw and Lexis. C.J.S. is available on Westlaw. Copies of both in print are generally available in most law libraries. Both national encyclopedias cover the same range of subjects but have distinctly different editorial choices. These choices make the encyclopedias complementary, not duplicative.

- C.J.S. uses comprehensive case citation theory, attempting to cite all relevant reported federal and state judicial opinions.
- Am Jur. employs a selected case citation process, citing to selected or seminal cases on the relevant topic.
- Am Jur. topics include more federal statutory materials than C.J.S.
- C.J.S. articles are more detailed than Am Jur. articles.
- C.J.S. includes more case citations than statutory citations.
- C.J.S. includes topic and key numbers to the West system.

In addition to national legal encyclopedias, states and regions may have a legal encyclopedia limited in scope by the jurisdiction. Sometimes these legal encyclopedias are also called *Jurisprudence*. If you are researching a question of state law, the contents of the state or regional legal encyclopedia are targeted to that jurisdiction and, as such, are especially helpful.

Examples of State Legal Encyclopedia or Jurisprudence
Georgia Jurisprudence
Strong's North Carolina Index
Michie's Jurisprudence of Virginia and West Virginia
Maryland Legal Encyclopedia
Pennsylvania Legal Encyclopedia

Figure 8.2 Examples of State Legal Encyclopedia or Jurisprudence

Legal encyclopedia entries are updated on a schedule set by the publisher. The print version will be updated by a system of pocket parts and pamphlets that supplement the information printed in the bound volume. A pocket part reflects its name. It is a thin pamphlet that is inserted into the pocket in the back of the volume.

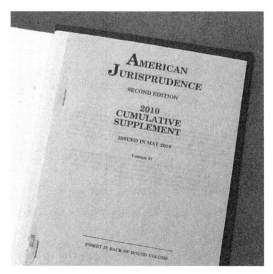

Figure 8.3 Pocket Part

When the information contained in the pocket part becomes so extensive that it does not fit, a separate pamphlet is published containing the current information. The pamphlet will be shelved beside the volume. If you are using an online instance of the encyclopedia, the information will be updated automatically to add the information collected at the time of the scheduled update. Look for the *"i"* *symbol* or source information to identify the currency of the online information.

Michie's Jurisprudence of Virginia & West Virginia   i

Figure 8.4 *"I" for Information for Michie's Jurisprudence on Lexis*

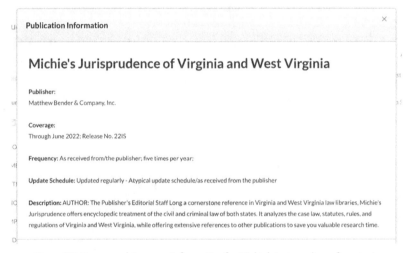

Figure 8.5 *Source and Currency Information for Michie's Jurisprudence from Lexis*

Use legal encyclopedias when:

1. You are unfamiliar with an area of the law.
2. You need to identify legal vocabulary for search terms
3. You need background information.
4. You need to obtain an introduction, general overview of the law, and a primary source as a starting point.

Caveat

Never cite to a legal encyclopedia. A legal encyclopedia is an excellent starting point but never an ending point.

Review What You've Read

1. When and for what purpose might a researcher use a legal encyclopedia?

2. What names might appear in the title to a legal encyclopedia?

3. What is the purpose of a pocket part?

Chapter 9

Restatements of Law

Characteristics of Restatements of Law

1. Overview of common law topics.
2. Provide a statement of black letter law in addition to commentary on the topic.
3. Contain examples and illustrations on the interpretation of the law.
4. Provide cross-references to primary authorities.
5. Are considered to carry substantial weight and be highly persuasive.
6. May be cited to a court.

Published by the American Law Institute, the Restatements attempt to create a statement of the idealized common law across all fifty states. The Restatements cover subjects such as Agency, Conflict of Laws, Contracts, Foreign Relations Law of the United States, Judgments, Property, Restitution, Security, Suretyship and Guaranty, The Law Governing Lawyers, Torts, Trusts, Unfair Competition, Employment Law, and Liability Insurance. A Restatement may include a statement reflecting what the scholars believe should be black letter law on the topic across the states and an emerging rule.

Black Letter Law Defined

A statement of a well-established legal rule from which there is no reasonable dispute.

The Restatements present a topic in a formulaic manner: (1) an initial statement of the specific rule of law; (2) followed by commentary on

the rule of law discussing the scope of application, meaning, and rationale of the rule; (3) illustrations taken from cases that demonstrate how
the law might be applied in a given instance; and (4) case summaries
applying and interpreting the law, which are arranged by jurisdiction
to assist the researcher. Finally, the most recent versions of the Restatements contain a section called *Reporter Notes*. Reporter Notes include a
history of the rule and references. The illustrations can be particularly
helpful in understanding the application of legal doctrine or how the
law applies.

1. Statement of the Rule of Law

§ 524 Contributory Negligence

Comment:
Reporter's Note
Case Citations - by Jurisdiction

(1) Except as stated in Subsection (2), the contributory negligence of the plaintiff is not a defense to the strict liability of one who carries on an abnormally dangerous activity.
(2) The plaintiff's contributory negligence in knowingly and unreasonably subjecting himself to the risk of harm from the activity is a defense to the strict liability.

↑ Back to top

Figure 9.1 §524 Contributory Negligence from Restatement

2. Commentary

Comment:

a. Since the strict liability of one who carries on an abnormally dangerous activity is not founded on his negligence, the ordinary contributory negligence of the plaintiff is not a defense to an action based on strict liability. The reason is the policy of the law that places the full responsibility for preventing the harm resulting from abnormally dangerous activities upon the person who has subjected others to the abnormal risk.

Figure 9.2 Commentary for §524 Contributory Negligence from Restatement

3. Illustration

Illustrations:
1. A, driving on the highway, attempts to pass a truck of the B Company on a narrow road. The truck is plainly marked "Danger, Dynamite," but A, being intent on the road and upon passing B, negligently fails to observe the sign. In passing, A negligently tries to drive through so narrow a space that he collides with the truck and causes the dynamite to explode. A's personal representative is not barred from recovery against B Company under a death statute.
2. The same facts as Illustration 1, except that A reads the sign. A's representative is barred from recovery.

Figure 9.3 Illustration from §524 Contributory Negligence from Restatement

4. Case Summary

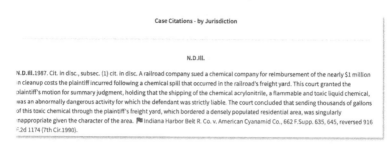

Case Citations - by Jurisdiction

N.D.Ill.

N.D.Ill.1987. Cit. in disc., subsec. (1) cit. in disc. A railroad company sued a chemical company for reimbursement of the nearly $1 million in cleanup costs the plaintiff incurred following a chemical spill that occurred in the railroad's freight yard. This court granted the plaintiff's motion for summary judgment, holding that the shipping of the chemical acrylonitrile, a flammable and toxic liquid chemical, was an abnormally dangerous activity for which the defendant was strictly liable. The court concluded that sending thousands of gallons of this toxic chemical through the plaintiff's freight yard, which bordered a densely populated residential area, was singularly inappropriate given the character of the area. Indiana Harbor Belt R. Co. v. American Cyanamid Co., 662 F.Supp. 635, 645, reversed 916 F.2d 1174 (7th Cir.1990).

Figure 9.4 Case Summary Associated with §524 Contributory Negligence from Restatement

The Restatements are written by members of the American Law Institute, whose membership consists of lawyers, law professors, and judges of recognized expertise. Restatements are authored by experts as demonstrated by professional achievement and interest in development of the law and therefore are highly persuasive. In certain select instances, a judge may take judicial notice of the Restatement's interpretation of the law, according such interpretation even greater persuasive weight. A Restatement is especially persuasive if you can cite a mandatory judicial opinion that adopts the view of the Restatement by judicial notice in your jurisdiction. In this instance, the correct citation is to the opinion taking judicial notice of the Restatement view.

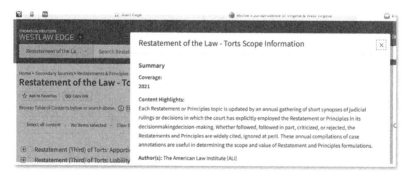

Figure 9.5 Scope and Information for Restatement from Westlaw

Restatement (Second) of Torts § 524 (1977)

Restatement of the Law - Torts   October 2021 Update
Restatement (Second) of Torts

*Figure 9.6   Currency Information for Restatement (Second)
of Torts §524 on Westlaw*

Use Restatements:

1. When the research question is a common law question.
2. To identify primary authority on topic.
3. To understand how the law is applied.
4. To locate the rule of law.

Review What You've Read

1. What value might a Restatement provide to the research process?

2. When researching what types of questions might the Restatement be uniquely helpful?

3. What weight does a Restatement carry?

Chapter 10

The Legal Periodical

Characteristics of the Legal Periodical

1. Generally written by experts (excluding the student note or comment).
2. Written with a specific focus on a narrow topic.
3. Contains depth of analysis on the topic.
4. Contains background information constituting a general overview and history of the topic.
5. Contains references to primary authority.
6. Critiques or advances the discussion of the state of the law on the specific topic.
7. Addresses matters of first impression or conflict in the law.
8. Addresses cutting-edge issues in the law.
9. May be cited to a court as persuasive authority.

The law review article, one type of legal periodical, consists of scholarly analysis on the current state of the law. Arguments as to advancement and interpretation of the law in addition to discussions of new developments are published in law reviews. A law review is typically published by a law school. In general, a law school will have a student-run law review that publishes articles on a general subject matter, known as a "flagship" publication. In addition to one or more specialty journals publishing on a specific topic, many schools also publish an online companion to their law review. The online companion often publishes shorter articles discussing current issues in the law.

Tip

I am in West Virginia researching an issue of West Virginia law, so the *West Virginia Law Review* is the journal I need. Not so fast. Geography is usually not a factor in the law review, especially flagship journals that publish articles across a wide variety of subjects. A law review in California may have published the definitive article on your subject. When searching for law review articles, cast a wide net.

Exception

The exception to the rule is the publication of a survey of recent judicial or legislative developments. Such surveys are best found in law reviews from law schools in the associated jurisdictions. For example: *The University of Richmond Law Review*, located in Richmond, Virginia, often devotes an issue to a survey of recent developments in Virginia law.

In addition to the student-run model, commercial publishers like the American Bar Association, Cambridge, and Oxford, also publish legal periodicals. Bar journals are distinguished from the traditional law review journal as practical short articles focusing on topics involving the real-life practice of law. Finally, legal newspapers like the *National Law Journal* or the *Daily Report* are also included in the legal periodical category.

Types of Legal Periodicals		
The Law Review	Student run, may also be called a law journal	Published by law schools, edited and managed by students containing notes, comments, essays, and expansive articles on a range of topics. May also include specialized journals on topics such as tax, intellectual property, or civil rights as examples.
The Law Review Online Companion	Student run	Published by law schools, edited, and managed by students containing articles, often shorter, on a wide range of topics of current interest.
The Law Review	Professionally produced by a commercial publisher, also called a law journal	Published by a commercial publisher, University or Scholarly Press, may be peer-reviewed, or edited by an expert.

Types of Legal Periodicals		
Bar Journal	Published by a state or local bar association	Published by a bar association on topics of interest to members of the bar. Focus is the practitioner.
Legal Newspaper	Professionally produced by a commercial publisher	Newspaper in concept and style with short articles on current and cutting-edge topics of interest to the legal profession.

Figure 10.1 Types of Legal Periodicals

The Law Review—Significance of Author and Persuasive Value		
Type of Author	*Description*	*Persuasive Value*
Legal Scholar	Article is authored by law professor or another expert. It generally addresses a problem or conflict in an area of law and proposes a solution.	Highest of the types of law reviews. Persuasive weight depends upon expertise of author, journal reputation, depth of analysis, and age of article.
Practitioner or Judge Authored	Article is written by one involved in the daily practice of law. Topics tend to suggest a judicial philosophy or provide practical advice as to an area of law. The depth of discussion and analysis is likely to be less than that of an article authored by a legal scholar. An excellent source for understanding an area of the law.	Less than that of the legal scholar, but still persuasive.
Student Authored Note or Comment	Authored by a law student, the topic is often a new case or statute. Excellent sources for background information and cross-references to primary authority.	Less persuasive than that of the law scholar.

Figure 10.2 The Law Review—Significance of Author and Weight

The law review article is an in-depth discussion of a specific topic. The law review article tends to follow a specific pattern of Introduction, Background, Discussion, Conclusion. The background section will contain a general overview of the topic, which is especially helpful to a researcher as it is a mini survey of the topic with reference to primary authorities.

Law review articles may be intentionally written to persuade an audience. Such articles may contain bias. Often a writer will use a law review article to advance an argument or theory for law reform, a new interpretation of a legal theory, or to fill a void—discussing a new area of the law or a new legal theory. Law reviews are great sources for policy arguments. Be discriminating in your use of persuasive arguments.

Law review articles and authors generally fall into one of three distinct categories: (1) article written by a legal scholar, (2) articles written by practitioners and judges, and (3) the student note or comment.

While you may not rely on a law review article as the sole basis of an argument, it may be cited to a court to buttress or flesh out an argument. The persuasive weight of the law review will depend upon the expertise of the author, depth of analysis and research, age of the article, and reputation of the journal.

Law review articles are current as of the date published. Unlike other secondary sources, there is no procedure to update the information. Take note of the date of publication as the law is continuously changing. This does not mean you cannot use older articles. Rather it means that the researcher should be diligent as to changes in the law impacting the persuasive value of the article.

Law reviews may be found in print in the law library collection or online. Westlaw and Lexis contain extensive databases of legal periodicals. Their databases tend to begin in the 1980s and come forward. It is important to check the scope and coverage of a database before searching. If you are conducting historical research or think that articles published prior to 1980 contain analysis relevant to your legal question, Westlaw and Lexis may not be the appropriate research platforms for your search. HeinOnline's Law Journal Library is a database that contains the full text of many legal materials. Most law libraries have subscriptions to this database that may be used on campus or off campus. If a law review is available in HeinOnline it is available from volume one of the series. On occasion, law reviews may be embargoed, meaning that the most recent issues may not be available for an agreed-upon length of time. If this is the case, the later volumes will be absent from the HeinOnline collection. The benefit of using HeinOnline to locate a legal periodical is the ability to see the full text of the article as it was published. Legal periodicals are but a fraction of the materials available in HeinOnline.

Use legal periodicals:

1. To identify policy arguments.

2. When your legal issue is cutting edge or novel.

3. To buttress an argument.

Review What You've Read

1. In what research circumstances might you find legal periodical articles helpful?

2. What is the currency of a legal periodical article?

3. Evaluate the statement, "Only current law review articles are useful."

Chapter 11

American Law Reports

Characteristics of an A.L.R. Annotation

1. Articles from the American Law Reports (A.L.R.) are known as annotations.
2. Collects all primary sources on a narrow point of law in one place.
3. Presents information organized to provide commentary and discussion on the universe of cases on a specific topic.
4. Lacks depth of analysis and commentary.
5. Not authored by experts.
6. Not appropriate for citation to a court.

A.L.R.eady done legal research is one way of thinking about *American Law Reports Annotations,* known as A.L.R. It is important to note that A.L.R. is its own unique source distinct from the legal encyclopedia and legal periodical. Initially begun as a competitor to the West reporter system, A.L.R. collected cases of note on a point of law. Issued in series, A.L.R. First is different in concept from the rest of A.L.R. A.L.R. First collected only selected cases viewed as seminal rather than all published cases. The West Reporter concept won out and A.L.R. evolved into the resource we see in the later series and today. Due to the age and the brevity of the annotation, researchers are advised to avoid A.L.R. and A.L.R.2d annotations.

A.L.R. Series
A.L.R.
A.L.R. 2d
A.L.R. 3d
A.L.R. 4th
A.L.R. 5th
A.L.R. 6th
A.L.R. Fed.
A.L.R. Fed. 2d

Figure 11.1 American Law Reports by Series

The article published in A.L.R. is called an annotation.[1] An annotation is an extensive collection of summaries of cases on one narrow point of law across multiple jurisdictions with minimal explanatory commentary. The goal is to collect all cases on that specific point, thus the label *A.L.R.eady done legal research*. The A.L.R. annotation is descriptive in content and specifically helpful to the researcher looking at the development of law across multiple jurisdictions or at the start of the research process for an overview of the topic and cross-references to primary, binding authority. A.L.R. annotations are also very narrow. They focus on a single point of law like—*Is a cat personal or real property?* A.L.R. is published in series 1–6, Fed., and Fed. 2d. A series is not to be confused with an edition that replaces or updates the annotations in the preceding series. Series are published sequentially with the annotations included in a series being superseded and made current by subsequently published annotations on the same topic published in a later series. A.L.R. is available in print in many law libraries and on Westlaw and Lexis. Online, the annotations are made current weekly by the addition of new cases.

---

1. The term *annotation* is used frequently in legal research. It is the name that refers to an A.L.R. article, it is the term that refers to the descriptive case summaries in a Digest and following the legislative text in an annotated code.

The ALR databases are made current by the weekly addition of relevant new cases.

Figure 11.2 Currency Statement for A.L.R. Annotation on Westlaw

A.L.R. annotations are usually not cited to a court, as the annotation is more descriptive than analytical in content and not authored by a noted expert. On occasion you may wish to cite to an annotation that summarized information such as the number of states recognizing a specific legal proposition.

Use an A.L.R. annotation:

1. When your research seeks to identify the law across multiple jurisdictions.
2. To locate primary authority.

Review What You've Read

1. When might an A.L.R. annotation be particularly useful to a research question?

2. What is the authority of an A.L.R. annotation?

3. Evaluate the statement—"A.L.R. annotations are highly persuasive as they are written by experts."

Chapter 12

Treatise

Characteristics of a Treatise

1. Comprehensive treatment on a specific topic like contracts.
2. Addresses the topic in a systematic manner.
3. Gathers statutes, regulations, and caselaw on a topic with commentary and explanation for context.
4. May consist of a single volume or multivolume set.
5. Addresses policy concerns.
6. Authored by an expert.
7. May be cited as persuasive authority to a court.

A treatise or book, sometimes also referred to as a monograph, is an in-depth treatment of a single area of law, such as contracts. Note, the word *treatise* will rarely appear in the title of a treatise. Written by an expert on the area of law, a treatise will gather all the relevant statutory provisions, regulations, and cases on the topic and present the primary authority in a thematic treatment accompanied by explanation and comment, providing a narrative discussion of the law. The treatise makes the law accessible to the researcher. Treatises also have audiences. *Am Jur. Trials* (not to be confused with Am Jur. the legal encyclopedia) and *Causes of Actions* are treatises geared toward the practitioner audience. They include checklists, forms, and examples of specific use to a practitioner. Sometimes these are referred to as practice materials. Other treatises are designed to appeal to the expert and be a substantive statement of the state of the law in that area. Examples of this type of treatise include *Powell on Real Property* or *Nimmer on Copyright*.

Tip

A treatise may be in print or online. In print, a treatise may be a single-volume book on a topic such as DUI in North Carolina or a multivolume set like Minor on Real Property in Virginia.

Use the library catalog to locate the treatises in your law library.

Treatises are available online and in print. If you are looking for a book in print, use the law library online catalog to locate a title. Once you are in the library stacks you can also browse the shelves to determine if there are other titles of interest since books on the same topic are shelved together. Online platforms like Westlaw and Lexis will vary in their collection of treatises, including only those published by their respective parent companies. Often, a title will only be available on one platform or another, depending on who published the treatise. Treatises are routinely updated, but the update interval varies widely based on the publisher and the author. In print, a pocket part or pamphlet may be used. Online the text is updated to include the current information. Like with the legal encyclopedia, the icon, "source information," scope note, or "publication information," will indicate the frequency of update and the currency of the information.

Goldstein on Copyright Scope Information   ⌐ ⌐
                                                                      ×
                                                                      ⌐ ⌐

Summary

Coverage:
Third Edition, 2021-2 Supplement

Content Highlights:
The 2021-2 Supplement to Goldstein on Copyright continues to follow the fast-breaking judicial, legislative, and regulatory developments in copyright law, providing intellectual property lawyers, entertainment lawyers, computer and technology lawyers, in-house counsel and business professionals with practical, up-to-date answers to all their questions concerning copyright issues.

Figure 12.1 Scope/Currency Information for Treatise on Westlaw

While the treatise is best used as a research tool, treatises are authored by experts and may be cited to a court as persuasive authority. The persuasive weight accorded to the source will depend upon the reputation of the author and the treatise.

Use a treatise:

1. When a detailed, specific discussion of the law is needed.
2. To locate primary authority on topic.
3. To locate citable persuasive authority to support your position.
4. To gain a better understanding of the law.

Review What You've Read

1. A legal treatise is particularly useful when researching what types of research questions?

2. Name two instances when a legal treatise will benefit the research process.

3. In evaluating the persuasive weight of a treatise, what is the primary indicia of weight?

Chapter 13

The Legal Dictionary, Publications for Law Students, and Finding Aids

A discussion of secondary sources is incomplete without mention of the legal dictionary, the hornbook, the nutshell, and the digest.

The legal dictionary is exactly what it seems. It is a dictionary specific to the law defining legal terms. The unique feature of the legal dictionary is that each word is defined with reference to a source. The best-known legal dictionary is *Black's Law Dictionary*, commonly known as *Black's*, but there are others. *Black's* is available in print and online via Westlaw. Words and phrases are arranged in alphabetical order. In addition to their definitions of legal terms, in recent years courts have relied upon dictionaries as a basis for statutory interpretation.

Words and Phrases Judicially Defined, commonly referred to as *Words and Phrases*, is a publication that takes the concept of a dictionary and combines it with the concept of a digest. For each case in which a judge defines a word or phrase, West creates a headnote capturing the definition. *Words and Phrases* collects all such headnotes, thus collecting all such words and phrases. *Words and Phrases* is a multivolume set arranged in alphabetical order first by word or phrase and then by jurisdiction. A researcher may search by a specific word or phrase and find its *judicially defined* meaning by jurisdiction. West has organized terms that have been defined within a judicial opinion and made them available in a dictionary-like format with the corresponding case citations. *Words and Phrases* is also available on Westlaw, although many find the print version easier to navigate. The print publication is updated by pocket part. For a research question that turns on the definition of a particular term, this set is particularly useful. *Words and Phrases* is one example of a *finding aid* or *finding tool.*

The hornbook is a derivative of the legal treatise. Of particular use by law students, the hornbook is effectively the legal textbook. The case-

book is the customary text for the law class. Casebooks contain highly edited visions of selected cases. The intent is for the law student to brief the case in preparation for a class where the professor will guide the student to an understanding of the law by asking questions based on the case. The hornbook contains narrative statements of the black letter law. Law students attempting to understand new concepts like *consideration* may find hornbooks to be useful.

Figure 13.1 Hornbook Cover from West Academic Hornbook Series

Like treatises, hornbooks are comprehensive treatments on the topics usually covered in a law school course. It is best to avoid citation to a hornbook; instead, look to a treatise on the same topic.

The nutshell is considered a study aid. It is a brief version of the hornbook. West publishes the Nutshell series, which is comprehensive in relation to the courses found in law schools. A Nutshell is a tool for the law student's use and not appropriate for citation to a court.

Figure 13.2 Cover of a Nutshell from West Academic Nutshell Series

Finding Aid Defined

A tool that assists the researcher in identification of other, particularly primary, sources. Finding aids are not authority, they are sources that aid the researcher. They are not citable to the court, but rather the underlying source is citable to the court.

The digest is a type of finding aid. Organized by jurisdiction, a digest is the *mother of all indices.* Arranged alphabetically by subject, the editors of the digest collect each headnote from a case and arrange the headnotes by subject. The digest is of particular significance due to stare decisis and precedent. Reliance on prior decisions makes finding decisions with the same factual predicate and legal issue key. The digest facilitates locating those precedential decisions. A digest is never cited as it is a collection of headnotes organized by subject matter. As you never cite to a headnote, you never cite to a digest entry. Digests are used to find primary, binding caselaw. While considered a secondary source, they are not considered persuasive.

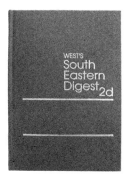

Figure 13.3 Southeastern 2d Digest

Summary Table of Secondary Sources			
Type	*Persuasive Value*	*Citable*	*Currency*
Legal Encyclopedia	None	No[1]	Regular intervals online and in print
Restatements	High	Yes	Annually by pocket parts and the inclusion of additional information online
Legal Periodical	Depends on author	Yes	As of date of publication
Treatise	Depends on author and publisher	Yes	Regular or infrequent interval online or in print
A.L.R. Annotation	Low	No[2]	Made current weekly online. Updated by subsequent annotations in print

Table continues on next page

---

1. I indicate that is not appropriate to cite to a legal encyclopedia. *Generally* might be an appropriate qualifier here. You can run an online search and find instances in which a state supreme court cites to a legal encyclopedia article in their opinion. There are even good reasons one might cite to an encyclopedia article such as when the language in a Wikipedia entry is the subject of the lawsuit. Despite the *generally* qualifier, I strongly suggest the best practice is to avoid citation to a legal encyclopedia. I suggest this is even a stronger statement for federal courts.

2. I indicate that it is not appropriate to cite to an A.L.R. annotation. *Generally* might be an appropriate qualifier here. You can run an online search and find instances in which a state

Table continued from last page

Summary Table of Secondary Sources			
Type	*Persuasive Value*	*Citable*	*Currency*
Law Dictionary	None—refer to the underlying source	Cite the underlying source	At publication of new edition in print
Words and Phrases	None	None	Pocket part in print
Digest	None	None	Pocket part, pamphlet, Advance Sheets in print
Hornbook	Low	None	New edition in print
Nutshell	None	None	New edition in print

Figure 13.4 Summary of Secondary Source Characteristics

Review What You've Read

1. What is the distinction among a legal treatise, a nutshell, and a hornbook?

2. What is a digest?

3. What authority is a finding tool or finding aid?

---

supreme court cites to an A.L.R. annotation in their opinion. There are even good reasons one might cite to an annotation, such as for the number of states taking a particular position of law. Despite the *generally* qualifier, I strongly suggest the best practice is to avoid citation to an A.L.R. annotation as they are not the product of expertise and substance. I suggest this is even a stronger statement for federal courts.

Chapter 14

The Citator

The citator is a tool unique in importance and function to legal research. It serves three purposes. The first purpose is to validate primary authority to confirm the law is currently *good law*.

Good Law Defined

Good law—(1) the law has not been changed or otherwise invalidated since it was published, (2) the case, statute, or regulation has not been accorded negative treatment of being criticized, overruled, overturned, amended, or repealed.

The second purpose is to identify how other courts apply your case by identifying the treatment or use by other courts. The third purpose is as a research tool identifying additional cases, statutes, and regulations related to a particular point of law. The citator as a research tool and the *one good case method* is discussed extensively in Part III.

Think of the law as a river constantly ebbing and flowing and changing its path. As the river changes it accretes, adding soil and land in its path. Similarly, the law is consistently accreting by adding new cases, statutes, and regulations. As new *stuff* is added, the new may impact the validity of the old. It may affirm that the law that existed in 1900 continues to be the law today or it may invalidate that law in favor of something new. Citators permit the researcher to look both forward and backward for information that considers the application of legal doctrine and to determine if the legal principle is still followed or curtailed. A researcher needs to ask the following questions:

1. What happened as the case was litigated to its conclusion? Did a higher court affirm the ruling of the lower court or reverse, remand, and/or modify?

2. Has the court or legislature changed its position over time, reversing itself and, thus, invalidating the primary authority?

3. How influential is this decision? Is the case followed by others? Is the position adopted by other jurisdictions? Is the point of law questioned, criticized, reversed, or overruled? Has the legislature acted to invalidate the law superseding the position by the enactment of a new statute? Are there new regulations updating or invalidating prior ones?

Specifically, a citator indicates if a source has been cited, the number of times the source is cited, and the treatment of a specific source by subsequent authority. Cases, statutes, and regulations live on after they become law. A case may comment on another case or interpret a statute or regulation. A statute may invalidate the current case law. Understanding how primary authority is subsequently treated is important due to the role of precedent in our legal system. Even if there is no negative treatment of the authority, identifying and understanding positive treatment is essential. This makes the citator uniquely important to legal research. Reliance on a precedent that is criticized or overruled is problematic for your client. A lawyer's failure to validate their primary authority as good law is malpractice.

Example

In *Climino v. Yale*, 638 F. Supp. 952, 959 n.7 (D. Conn. 1986), the court took the unusual step of noting it was unable to discern whether sloppy research or warped advocacy tactics were responsible for errors of omission, admonishing corporation Counsel that diligent research, includes Shepardizing cases, and is a professional responsibility.[1]

---

1. Climino v. Yale, 638 F. Supp. 952, 959 n.7 (D. Conn. 1986).

There are multiple examples of citators; however, there are two legal citators that lawyers commonly rely upon—Shepard's Citations (known as Shepard's), available in print and on Lexis, and KeyCite, available on Westlaw. *Shepardize* is a verb meaning to confirm your primary authority is good law using Shepard's Citator. In 1873 Frank Shepard began publishing lists of citations to Illinois Supreme Court opinions on gummed paper for attorneys to place in the margins of their bound reporters. This evolved to the book version known as Shepard's. Coverage quickly expanded beyond Illinois to include all states and the federal courts. While Shepard's is available in print, the update process for the print makes it out of date before it can be printed and many law libraries have discontinued their print subscriptions to Shepard's Citations in favor of the online instance of Shepard's on Lexis.

When to Use a Citator
1. Both during and at the conclusion of the research process to locate additional authority.
2. To validate the status of every piece of primary authority cited.
3. To identify and better understand how other courts are using your authority.

Figure 14.1 When to Use a Citator

Understanding the terminology and process used with citators is key. When validating your case as good law you will be evaluating a list of subsequently decided cases that cite to your *original* case. The *original* case is the starting point, the subject of the citator search. A *citing case* or *citing source* is a case or source that cites to your original case. For example, you just found and read *Rice v. Paladin Enterprises, Inc.*, 128 F.3d 233 (4th Cir. 1997) This is the *original case*. You review the citator report and locate *Smithfield Foods, Inc. v. United Food and Commercial Workers International Union*, 584 F. Supp. 2d 838 (E.D. Va. 2008) in which the Eastern District of Virginia distinguishes the ruling in *Rice v. Paladin*. *Smithfield* is referred to as the *citing case*.

Direct and indirect case history are concepts in the interpretation of the citator report. Direct history refers to all the judicial opinions issued in a single matter. For example, you file suit in the Eastern District of Virginia. You lose at the trial court and appeal to the Fourth Circuit.

Figure 14.2 Citator Diagram

The Fourth Circuit remands your matter back to the Eastern District of Virginia for reconsideration. The decisions at each stage from the Eastern District of Virginia and the Fourth Circuit would be *direct history*. Any opinion issued after the original opinion is referred to as *subsequent history*. An opinion issued before the original opinion is called *prior history*. In our example, the opinion from the Eastern District of Virginia is the original opinion so the opinion from the Fourth Circuit is considered subsequent history.

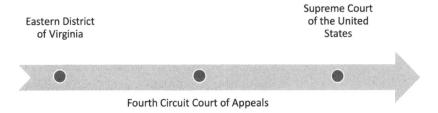

Figure 14.3 Citator/Court Diagram

Let's change things up. If the opinion from the Fourth Circuit Court of Appeals is the original opinion, the opinion from the Eastern District of Virginia becomes prior history. An opinion based on an appeal to the Supreme Court of the United States would be *subsequent direct history*. *Indirect history* refers to an unrelated case that cites the original case.

Direct and indirect history may be positive, negative, or neutral. Positive treatments include actions such as affirming the decision. Negative treatments include actions such as reversal, overturning, questioning, criticism. Neutral actions are those with neither a positive nor a negative connotation.

Citator Treatment	Positive Treatment	Negative Treatment	Neutral
Citing case disagrees with the reason in the original case		Criticized	Criticized
Citing case is different in law or fact from original case		Distinguished	Distinguished
The original case is interpreted in a significant way	Explained	Explained	Explained
Citing case refers to original case as controlling authority	Followed		
An inconsistency between the citing case and the original case is explained and shown not to exist	Harmonized	Harmonized	Harmonized
Dissenting opinion			Dissent
Citing case refuses to extend the holding of the original case beyond application of the original holding	Limited	Limited	Limited
Ruling in the original case is expressly overruled by the citing case		Overruled	Overruled
Citing case questions the continuing validity or precedential value of the original case		Questioned/ Validity questioned	Abrogated as stated in by questionable precedent

Table continues on next page

Table continued from last page

Citator Treatment	Positive Treatment	Negative Treatment	Neutral
Statute amended	Amended	Amended	Amended
New section added to statute	Addition	Addition	Addition
Provisions of existing statute abrogated		Repealed	
New legislation substituted for language of existing statute	Superseded	Superseded	Superseded
Validity of statute	Constitutional/ Valid	Unconstitutional/ Valid questioned by/Void or invalid by	Void or invalid by questionable precedent/Valid depublished

Figure 14.4 Citator Treatment

On Westlaw and Lexis, citator information is available at the top of the page next to the identifying information for the source. Consider the example of the case *Owasso Independent School District v. Falvo*, 534 U.S. 426 (2002).

Figure 14.5 Citator Tabs on Westlaw

Westlaw uses a system of colored flags[2] and Lexis a system of colored signals to indicate treatment.

2. https://legal.thomsonreuters.com/blog/westlaw-tip-of-the-week-checking-cases-with-keycite/.

🏴 A *red flag* warns that the case is no longer good law for at least one of the points of law it contains. For instance, the decision was reversed on appeal or overturned years later by a decision of the same court.

🏴 A *yellow flag* warns that the case has some negative history but has not been reversed or overruled. For example, the reasoning of the decision was criticized or its holding was limited to a specific set of facts.

🏴 A *blue-striped flag* warns that the case has been appealed to the U.S. Court of Appeals or the U.S. Supreme Court (excluding appeals originating from agencies).

Figure 14.6 Westlaw Citator Signals

On Westlaw you can quickly identify the yellow caution flag indicating further investigation is needed. Navigate between the tabs of the KeyCite report across the top of the page labeled "Negative Treatment," "History," and "Citing Reference" to locate the relevant authority. Clicking on the negative treatment tab provides a report of subsequent authorities indicating negative treatment of the original source. Specifically, negative treatment means the original source is negatively impacted by events or decisions in the cases referenced by the citations. Here three cases are cited suggesting negative indirect history. The negative treatment is described in the "treatment" column of the chart and the depth of discussion is indicated by green bars in the *depth* column of the chart.

Figure 14.7 KeyCite Report on Westlaw

The newest addition to KeyCite is the implicit overrule warning. This is a recent addition and reflects the instance when a case is overruled but that case is not the case you relied upon. The orange circle with a white triangle and an exclamation point warns the researcher of this.

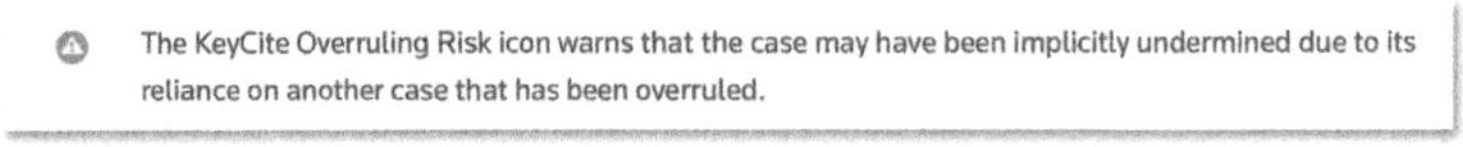

> ⚠   The KeyCite Overruling Risk icon warns that the case may have been implicitly undermined due to its reliance on another case that has been overruled.

Figure 14.8 KeyCite Overruling Risk Icon

What does implicit risk of overruling mean? For purposes of illustration, you want to cite to *Winters* for a specific point of law. *Winters* relies on *Sanders* for the point of law that you wish to use. *Thompson* explicitly overrules the *Sanders* decision on your point of law but did not overrule *Winters*. As *Winters* was not explicitly addressed in the *Thompson* decision, it has no negative treatment even though the point of law it relies on is overruled. The implicit risk flag makes the researcher aware of the risk of reliance. This also begs a best practice for research. Drill down to the original case with the language you like. You should do this not only due to the risk of implicit overruling but also because mistakes happen, and language that is incorrectly cited in one case may be picked up in subsequent cases preserving the mistake.

Signal	Meaning
● Red Stop Sign	**Warning - Negative treatment indicated** - indicates that citing references in the *Shepard's* Citations Service contain strong negative history or treatment of your case (e.g., overruled by or reversed).
① Red Exclamation Mark in a White Circle	**Warning** - indicates that citing references for a statute in the *Shepard's* Citations Service contain strong negative treatment of the section (e.g., the section may have been found to be unconstitutional or void).
Ｑ White Q in an Orange Square	**Questioned: Validity questioned by citing reference** - indicates that the citing references in the *Shepard's* Citations Service contain treatment that questions the continuing validity or precedential value of your case because of intervening circumstances, including judicial or legislative overruling as mentioned in the citing reference.
▲ Yellow Triangle	**Caution: Possible negative treatment indicated** - indicates that citing references in the *Shepard's* Citations Service contain history or treatment that may have a significant negative impact on your case (e.g., limited or criticized by).
◆ White Plus Sign in a Green Diamond	**Positive treatment indicated** - indicates that citing references in the *Shepard's* Citations Service contain history or treatment that has a positive impact on your case (e.g., affirmed or followed by).
Ⓐ White A in a Blue Circle	**Citing references with analysis available** - indicates that citing references in the *Shepard's* Citations Service contain treatment of your case that is neither positive nor negative (e.g., explained).
❶ White I in a Blue Circle	**Citation information available** - indicates that citing references are available in the *Shepard's* Citations Service for your case, but the references do not have history or treatment analysis (e.g., the references are law review citations).

Figure 14.9 Shepard's Signals[3]

Shepard's on Lexis functions similarly. The symbols are unique to the system.

Citator information will vary between Shepard's and KeyCite due to the different methods for identifying and evaluating subsequent authorities and different policies underlying each system. The Shepard's report for *Owasso* is below and, like the KeyCite report, suggests further action be taken by the researcher to identify the potential negative treatment due to the caution signal indicated by use of the yellow triangle.

Figure 14.10 Shepard's Display

3. https://lexisnexis.custhelp.com/app/answers/answer_view/a_id/1088155/~/Shepard's-signals-and-analysis.

The Shepard's citator report has a different structure from that of the KeyCite report. First negative treatment is not differentiated in the initial tab. The researcher must first navigate to the "citing decisions" tab. From there you may narrow by type of subsequent treatment: caution, positive, and neutral treatment.

Figure 14.11 Shepard's Report—Lexis

No matter the signals or flags assigned in a citator report, researchers are required to continue their research by investigating the additional authorities. Negative signals or flags are not an absolute bar to using the information without further investigation. Most cases contain multiple points of law. All it takes is one point of law receiving negative treatment by one subsequent authority to trigger or generate a red flag or stop signal. Your responsibility upon noting negative treatment is to identify the authority that triggers the negative treatment, locate that authority, identify and analyze the language resulting in the negative treatment, and determine if the subsequent authority invalidates the point of law in the case you wish to cite. When the subsequent citing authority is confirmed to invalidate the point of law, that law is no longer *good law*. What if the point of law that results in a caution flag is not relevant to your legal question? Then you remain free to use the case in support of your point of law. For example, you wish to cite to *Owasso* in support of the prop-osition that a peer-graded assignment is not a student record within the definition of an educational record under the Family Educational Rights and Privacy Act, or FERPA. While there are three cases that indicate neg-ative treatment in *Owasso* and those cases discuss different aspects of an educational record, you note that those cases do not negatively impact the statement in *Owasso* that a peer-graded assignment is not protected under FERPA. As the negative treatment is on a different point of law, it remains acceptable to cite to *Owasso* for this point of law despite the yellow signal.

As one of the key functions of a legal citator is to confirm continuing validity of your primary authority, understanding when a source ceases to be *good law* is critical. There are three instances in which a case ceases to be good law.

1. The subsequent direct history of the case contains an adverse ruling by a higher court. In other words, on appeal the decision in the original case is reversed or modified.

2. Subsequent indirect history contains cases from the same ju-risdiction with adverse treatment. More simply stated, in an-other case involving different parties the law in the original case is overruled, modified, reversed, questioned, or criticized. Generally, this happens over time when policy moves the law by distinguishing the application of the law in earlier cases or refusing to apply the law in the same manner.

3. The law in the opinion is negatively impacted by another source of law. Typically, this occurs when new legislation changes the law.

Review What You've Read

1. Name two purposes served by a citator.

2. Identify two examples of types of information that the citator could provide that would cause you to believe a case is no longer good law.

3. Describe three instances in which a point of law becomes *bad law*.

Review What You've Read Part II—
Secondary Sources and Finding Aids

1. Describe four situations in which you should begin your research with a secondary source.

2. For each of the resources listed below, name the secondary source that fits the description.

   a. A source used to provide general background information and limited citations to primary authority but no in-depth analysis of a topic.

   b. A source selected to provide an in-depth discussion and some analysis of an area of law and for citations to primary authority.

   c. A source that provides an overview of an area of law, citations to primary and secondary authorities, policy, or other arguments to resolve a conflict in the law or information on an undeveloped area of law.

   d. A source that collects case summaries from a variety of jurisdictions and provides an overview of the law on the topic.

   e. A source that restates the common law.

3. For each of the secondary sources listed below, provide two or three descriptive phrases that distinguish the source from the others.

   a. Treatise

   b. Encyclopedia

   c. Legal periodical article

   d. Restatements of the Law

   e. *American Law Reports* (A.L.R. annotation)

Part III

Search Strategies

LEARNING OBJECTIVES

1. Create and implement effective terms and connector search statements.
2. Effectively use pre- and post-search filters to narrow result sets.
3. Navigate an index by using search terms brainstormed in a research plan to locate a relevant source.
4. Use tables of contents to navigate a source to find relevant material within.
5. Use a Popular Name Table to locate statutes.
6. Retrieve a citator report on either Westlaw or Lexis.
7. Use a citator report to expand research to related primary and secondary sources.
8. Understand the purpose of a digest in the legal research process.
9. Navigate the Topic & Key Number System on Westlaw Edge to find relevant cases.

Strategies to Locate Information Efficiently and Effectively

Finding legal information is more than typing a question into Google. Your goal is to locate specific information that answers your client's legal question efficiently and effectively. Too often a researcher takes what appears to be the best of the first three search results on the page and runs with it. Often that source is not the best fit, it is not authoritative, is incomplete, or is not current. Fortunately, legal information is highly organized. Making use of the tools created to facilitate finding relevant information efficiently and effectively can make the legal research process much easier. Research is expensive as it involves the expenditure of time. As an attorney your time is valuable. In many law firms, time is billed in six-minute intervals. Whether you account by the billable hour or a flat fee, spending time going down a rabbit hole just to miss the controlling authority is wasteful. The remainder of this text explores the different tools and strategies available to lawyers to assist in locating good information in a timely, efficient, and effective manner. Specifically, understanding how and when to employ the search strategies of: (1) find by citation, (2) find by cross-reference, (3) use of an index, (4) use of a Table of Contents, (5) search using the Popular Names Table, (6) search by citator, (7) search by Topic and Key Number, (8) search by terms and connectors and (9) compiling a legislative history.

Westlaw and Lexis are examples of research platforms with many databases. Like Google, Westlaw and Lexis make use of a global search box on the home page. This is an all-too-inviting option for searching. Searches from the global search box search all databases on the platform, all sources, and all types of authority, and produce thousands of results. This is a useful tool and strategy for locating a single source or finding a known item but not for efficient and effective searching. The nine search strategies detailed in this part are targeted strategies that narrow and refine your result sets for efficient and effective research.

Chapter 15

Find by Citation and
Find by Cross-Reference

Find by citation and find by cross-reference are two of the most direct searches a researcher can employ. The prerequisite is that you have existing information on which to build. This information can come to the researcher in any number of ways. A partner may provide you with a citation to a case, statute, regulation, law review, or another source. You may be deep into the research process and locate a source that references another source that looks promising. The premise of *find by citation* or *find by cross-reference* is that you are building on the information you already possess. Think of this as adding a link to a chain.

Find by citation or cross-reference is generally thought of as a search strategy used in online research platforms, but it can also be effectively used with print materials. The strategy is to use known information, the citation, to locate another relevant source.

As an example, Senior Partner is working on an issue of federal tax treatment that involves the definition of a private foundation within the context of nonprofits. They ask for your assistance and provide you with a citation to a judicial opinion: *Change-All Souls Housing Corp. v. United States*, 671 F.2d 463 (1982). Since you have the citation, you can easily retrieve the opinion directly or in print in the volumes of the Federal Reporter, Second Series (F.2d) or online using the find by citation search strategy. In print, you can locate the opinion in the Federal Reporter, Second Series, using the volume and page number in the citation. Online in either Westlaw or Lexis, you may locate the case by simply typing

Figure 15.1 Find by Citation

"671 F2d 463" into the global search bar and clicking the orange search button. The result will pull up the case.

Now you have the opinion Senior Partner mentioned. Using the find by cross-reference search strategy you can build on the information you already have. Recall your goal is to determine the definition of "private foundation" for nonprofits in the context of federal tax. In the first paragraph of the opinion, you find mention of a section of the federal statutes. Here, 26 U.S.C. §509(a).

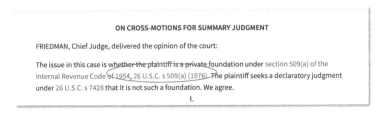

Figure 15.2 Find by Cross-Reference

Online in Westlaw and Lexis, the statutory section is linked. Using that link you can go directly to the section of the code that provides the statutory definition of a private foundation. This is the find by cross-reference search strategy.

Figure 15.3 Relevant Section from U.S.C.A.

In print or if a source is not linked you would still use the citation given as a cross-reference, but you will have to retrieve the second source by its citation to locate the authority.

Stop and consider how quickly you located the relevant primary authority using these two strategies—*find by cross-reference* and *find by citation*. In two steps you have a relevant judicial opinion and the code section that defines the private foundation for tax purposes. This is what is meant by effective and efficient searching. For purposes of comparison, consider the screenshot below of a Google search for "private foundation." While Google is a powerful tool, here it fails to home in on the relevant legal information found with the strategies of find by citation and find by cross-reference.

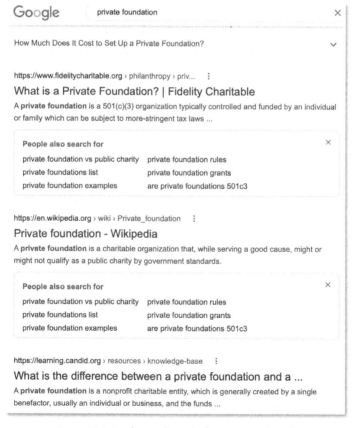

Figure 15.4 Google Search Results "Private Foundation"

A final note on *find by citation* and *find by cross-reference*: these strategies presume familiarity with legal citation such as knowledge of common reporter, code, and secondary source abbreviations. Familiarity with such abbreviations will come as you practice formulating your own legal citations. Until you achieve that baseline familiarity, keeping the *Bluebook* nearby may be helpful.

Review What You've Read

1. In your own words, describe the search strategies of *find by citation* and *find by cross-reference*.

2. When should you use the strategy of *find by citation*?

3. Knowledge of what assists the researcher in using the research strategies of *find by citation* and *find by cross-reference*?

Chapter 16

The Index and Table of Contents

As previously mentioned, legal information is highly organized to facilitate the discovery of information. Two of the common tools used to make information findable are the index and the table of contents. While these features were traditional in the print world, they persist in online research platforms such as Westlaw and Lexis. The use of an index or table of contents as a search strategy is tailored to certain types of resources. In particular, legal encyclopedias, treatises, and codes have indexes and tables of contents that classify information by subject, making it easier to locate using search terms from your research plan.

Index and Table of Contents Defined

Index—*list reflecting a sequential or topical arrangement of material usually in alphabetical order with page references directing the user to specific information. An index may be located in the back of a work, as a separate volume in a series, or as part of an online presentation of a work.*

Table of Contents—*a list of divisions, usually chapters or titles, and the corresponding location of where the information begins. Traditionally appearing at the beginning of a book or work and reflecting the structure or parts of the work.*

Should I Use an Index or Table of Contents if My Source Is:
A legal treatise
A code
A legal encyclopedia

Figure 16.1 Use an Index or Table of Contents—When?

Using either the index or table of contents is likely a familiar strategy, one you already have used to navigate non-legal information. These tools are available in texts of all kinds, including those as common as a cookbook. Indexes and tables of contents classify the information in the source based on commonly used terms that should be familiar to the user. They break the concepts discussed into granular or bite-sized pieces of information. As between the index and the table of contents, the table of contents will reflect the chapters and, as appropriate, subheadings as determined by the author. Just remember, you are searching a smaller universe of information that is specifically targeted rather than the entire database or platform.

Implement this search strategy using the following steps:

   a. Identify your source and confirm it is one appropriate for this search strategy.
   b. Locate the index or table of contents.
   c. Review your search terms from your research plan and select the ones likely to be found in either the index or the table of contents.
   d. Find the term in the index or table of contents and note the corresponding location of the information in the source.
   e. Locate the information and evaluate it for use in your legal research.

Using the table of contents online—American *Jurisprudence 2d* on Lexis—Example:

As an example, look for information regarding a *gift causa mortis* on Lexis using a legal encyclopedia. A *gift causa mortis* is a property concept referring to a gift made in contemplation of imminent death. Your client's issue depends on the interpretation of the immediacy of death requirement. You select the national legal encyclopedia *American Jurisprudence 2d or Am. Jur.* on Lexis for your search. Using the global search box on the homepage, you type American Jurisprudence or Am. Jur. and select the title as your source from the drop-down menu that appears as you type. After clicking the title, the next page displays the table of contents for the source. Reflecting on your research plan you determine *gift* is the broad subject matter relevant to your legal question. You browse the table of contents to find the topic *gift*. Using the + sign to further expand the topic, you identify the subtopic of *gifts inter vivos and gifts causa mortis distinguished.* Again, using the + sign to expand the topic further, you note the section on *expectation of donor's death.* Selecting that topic, the link takes you to the individual encyclopedia entry discussing the requirement of death as an element of a gift causa mortis.

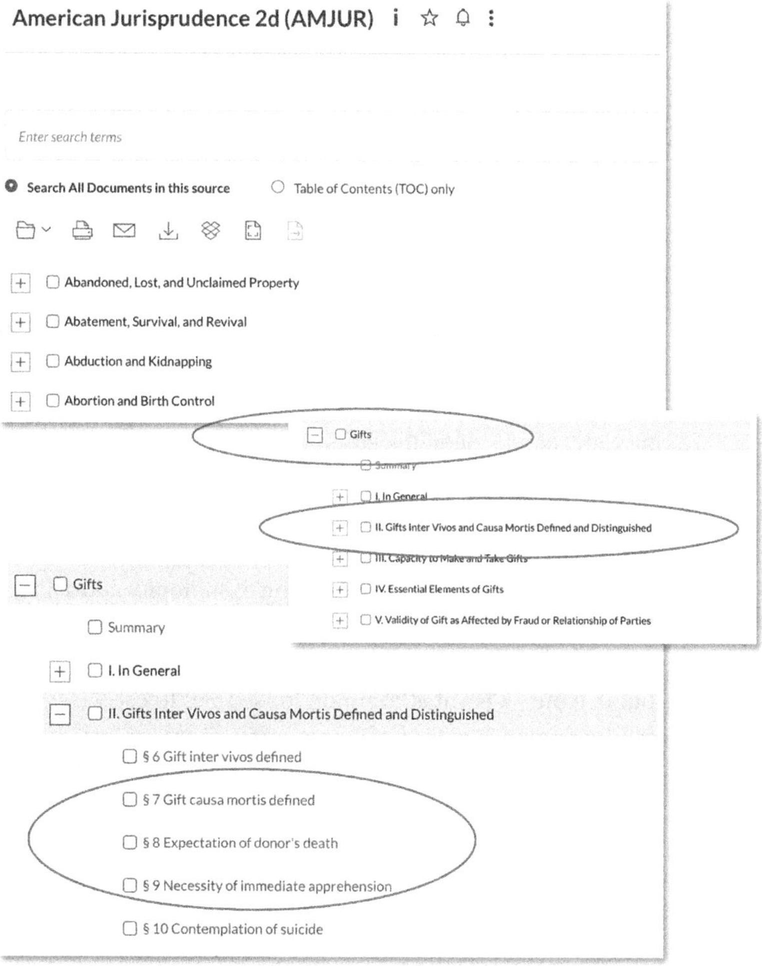

Figure 16.2 Table of Contents Search Am. Jur. on Lexis

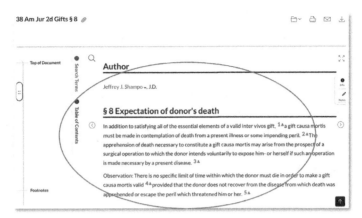

Figure 16.3 Am. Jur. Expectation of Donor's Death/Table of Contents Search

Using an index online—Strong's North Carolina Index on West-law—Example:

> *Strong's North Carolina Index* is the state legal encyclopedia for North Carolina. Note the name does not include either juris-prudence or encyclopedia. Encyclopedia names vary by juris-diction. Available on Westlaw, *Strong's North Carolina Index* has both a table of contents feature on the landing page and an index. The index is found in the Tools & Resources section on the right-hand side of the landing page. Navigate the index by browsing the alphabetical list across the top of the page or us-ing a keyword search. Selecting *g* for gifts, you will find *gifts and donations* among the topics. Selecting *gifts and donations* leads to an even more granular listing of subtopics and a listing for *causa mortis gifts* along with references to specific sections of the encyclopedia where detailed information on the topic is found. Note, in law it is common for sources to use § (section) or ¶ (paragraph) instead of a page number as a pointer for the location of information. This is due to the method used to pe-riodically update sources to provide the most current, up-to-date information possible. Use of the section or paragraph symbol permits the addition of new material without the need for repagination of the work.

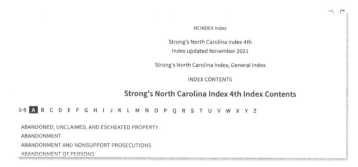

Figure 16.4 Index Search Strong's North Carolina Index

The search strategy of using an index or a table of contents to locate information is an efficient and effective tool, particularly when you have a strong search vocabulary from your research plan. The index identifies and groups information by topic. All the researcher needs to do is identify the appropriate search term, locate that term, and quickly drill down to the relevant text. This method is particularly effective with the secondary sources of legal encyclopedias and treatises. Not all sources include indexes or tables of contents. Understanding which sources have this feature is key.

In addition to certain secondary sources, using a table of contents or index search for statutory research is particularly effective. A judge writing a judicial opinion tends to write in a narrative format and uses descriptive words. By contrast, legislatures drafting provisions for a statute tend to use highly prescriptive language that leans towards being technical and abstract as needed to cover a variety of situations. The use of technical and abstract language makes full-text searching of statutes inefficient and index or table of contents searching highly efficient.

Using an Index to a Code—United States Code Annotated on Westlaw—Example:

> You represent a winery in Virginia that wishes to ship wine to customers outside the Commonwealth of Virginia. Your client asks, which federal laws govern direct shipment of wine? Using Westlaw, you locate the United *States Code Annotated* (U.S.C.A.), either by typing the title in the global search bar on

the homepage or by selecting "Statute & Court Rules" from the "Content types" menu, then choosing U.S.C.A. Find the index in the "Tools and Resources" section on the right-hand side of the page. From the index landing page, select *w* to locate *wines* or type *wines* into the search box at the top of the page. Note that typing a term into the search box at this point searches only index terms.

Figure 16.5 Index Search U.S.C.A.

Selecting *wines* retrieves a list of subtopics that consists of a smaller and focused list of options. The list of options includes *direct shipment* and a link to the relevant section of the code.

§ 124. Direct shipment of wine

27 USCA § 124 · United States Code Annotated · Title 27. Intoxicating Liquors · Effective: November 2, 2002 (Approx. 2 pages)

Document   Notes of Decisions (0)   History (86) ▾   Citing References (29) ▾   Context & Analysis (0) ▾   ⟷ Fulls

Table of Contents   ⟨ § ⟩   Outline   🔍 🏷 📘▾ 🔔 ∞▾ 📁 ⬇

United States Code Annotated
  Title 27. Intoxicating Liquors
    Chapter 6. Transportation in Interstate Commerce

Effective: November 2, 2002

27 U.S.C.A. § 124

§ 124. Direct shipment of wine

Currentness

(a) Conditions for transporting certain wine

During any period in which the Federal Aviation Administration has in effect restrictions on airline passengers to ensure safety, the direct shipment of wine shall be permitted from States where wine is purchased from a winery, to another State or the District of Columbia, if--

(1) the wine was purchased while the purchaser was physically present at the winery;

(2) the purchaser of the wine provided the winery verification of legal age to purchase alcohol;

Figure 16.6 U.S.C.A. Result Using Index

Using the Table of Contents to a Code—United States Code Service on Lexis—Example:

> Continuing with our example of *direct shipment of wine across state lines*, you wish to locate the federal statutory provision governing this action using the federal code on Lexis. The United States Code Service (U.S.C.S.) is the Lexis version of the federal code. It is an unofficial, annotated version of the federal code. Using Lexis, you locate the U.S.C.S. either by typing the title in the global search bar on the homepage or by selecting "Statutes & Legislation" from the "Content" tab, then selecting "Federal" from the list of jurisdictions. Finally, choose U.S.C.S.—*United States Code Service—Titles 1 through 54*. This next page is the table of contents for the U.S.C.S.

From this page you might select agriculture, as wine is a product of growing grapes; however, a quick scan or browse of the table of contents entries also reveals "Title 27 Intoxicating Liquors" as an option. Given that wine is an alcoholic beverage, you expand this topic, clicking on the + symbol, and find "Chapter 6. Transportation in Interstate Commerce."

Figure 16.7 U.S.C.S. Index Search

As this appears to be directly on target, again you expand by clicking on the + symbol to locate the reference to the specific section of the code: §124 Direct shipment of wine.

☐ TITLE 27. INTOXICATING LIQUORS (§§ 1 – 228)

    ☐ Preceding § 1

    ☐ CHAPTER 1. GENERAL PROVISIONS [REPEALED] (§§ 1 – 5)

    ☐ CHAPTER 2. PROHIBITION OF INTOXICATING BEVERAGES [REPEALED, OMITTED, OR TRANSFERRED] (§§ 11 – 64)

    ☐ CHAPTER 2A. BEER, ALE, PORTER, AND SIMILAR FERMENTED LIQUOR [REPEALED OR OMITTED] (§§ 64a – 64p)

    ☐ CHAPTER 3. INDUSTRIAL ALCOHOL [OMITTED OR SUPERSEDED] (§§ 71 – 90a)

    ☐ CHAPTER 4. PENALTIES [REPEALED] (§§ 91 – 92)

    ☐ CHAPTER 5. PROHIBITION REORGANIZATION ACT OF 1930 [REPEALED] (§§ 101 – 108)

    ☐ CHAPTER 6. TRANSPORTATION IN INTERSTATE COMMERCE (§§ 121 – 124)

        ☐ § 121. State statutes as operative on termination of transportation; original packages

        ☐ § 122. Shipments into States for possession or sale in violation of State law

        ☐ § 122a. Injunctive relief in Federal district court

        ☐ § 122b. General provisions

        ☐ § 123. [Repealed]

        ☐ § 124. Direct shipment of wine

Figure 16.8 U.S.C.S. Index Search — Wine

Indexes and tables of contents are tools that use the existing classification systems of legal information and locate highly relevant information efficiently.

Review What You've Read

1. What types of sources lend themselves to a table of contents or index search?

2. What part of the research planning process is useful in using a table of contents or index search?

Chapter 17

Researching Using the
Popular Names Table

The Popular Names Table is a search tool unique to statutory research using a code. This tool is available for codes on Westlaw, Lexis, and in print. In print the popular names table is often found at the end of the code. It may appear as a separate appendix or volume before or after the general index. The popular names table is a table associated with a single code that connects the commonly known *popular name* or an act with citations to the title, chapter, and sections in the code. A popular name may describe the legislation or the authors.

Using the United States Code Annotated on Westlaw—Example:

You represent a land developer interested in raising the elevation of marshland to develop a new housing complex. Your client is concerned about whether marshland is considered a *navigable waterway* within the Clean Water Act. Therefore, you wish to locate the applicable definition of *navigable water* in the Clean Water Act.

Using Westlaw, you locate the U.S.C.A., either by typing the title in the global search bar on the homepage or by selecting "Statutes & Court Rules" from the "Content types" menu, then choosing U.S.C.A. Find the *Popular Names Table* in the "Tools & Resources" section on the right-hand side of the page.

From the landing page for the *Popular Names Table,* use the alphabetical list across the top of the page and select *C*. From the *C*s, locate Clean Water Act.

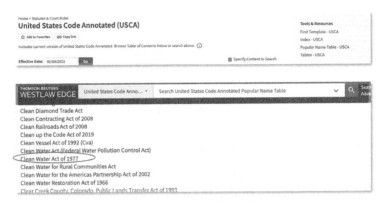

Figure 17.1 Popular Names Table Search—U.S.C.A.

Note, there are several options of *Clean Water*. When in doubt, opt for the one that appears closest to the popular name by which you know the statute. Here *Clean Water Act (Federal Water Pollution Control Act)* is the relevant act. Following the link for the *Clean Water Act* takes you to a chart identifying all the places in the code where provisions of the act were codified. Note that the U.S.C.A. citations are linked.

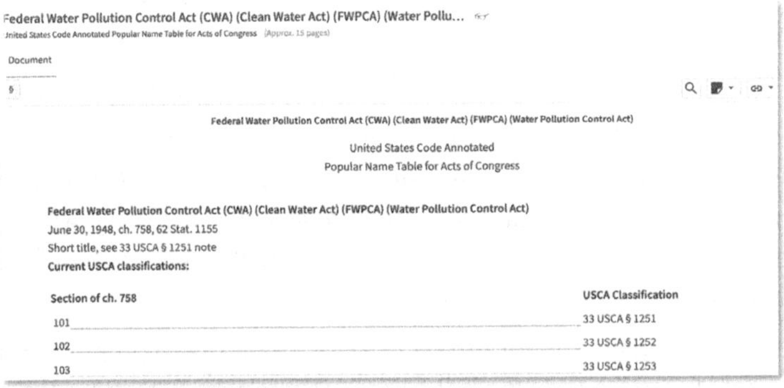

Figure 17.2 Popular Names Table—U.S.C.A.

The size and complexity of the act will determine the number of places in the code where parts of the act are found. After a bit of trial and error you determine the relevant language is found in section 502 of the act.

Figure 17.3 Popular Names Table—U.S.C.A. §502 Example

Selecting the link to 33 U.S.C.A. §1362 highlights a definitional section that contains subpart (7) with the definition of *navigable waters* for purposes of the Clean Water Act.

Figure 17.4 Popular Names Table—Statute

The benefit of the Popular Names Table as a search strategy is that it associates the commonly used name of a statute as passed by the legislature with sections of the code where the act is organized by subject.

Review What You've Read

1. The Popular Names Table search strategy is limited to what resource(s)?

2. When and why is the Popular Names Table search strategy particularly useful?

3. Evaluate the following statement: The Popular Names Table search strategy is only available for online federal codes.

Chapter 18

Researching with Citators

Chapter 14 discusses the three functions of a citator. The first function is to confirm the continuing validity of a primary authority. The second function is to identify the treatment of your case by other courts. The third function of a citator is to serve as a research tool to identify additional sources. The citator identifies other sources that cite to this authority on the same principle of law demonstrating the relevance of the citing source. Think of the citator report as generating an entire list of cross-references to relevant authority,

Shepard's and KeyCite *Heller v. Somdahl*—Example:

Your client comes to you wishing to sue his best friend for *alienation of affection*. For the purposes of this example, your jurisdiction is North Carolina. The story your client shares is that of a long and loving marriage until two years ago. At that time an alleged affair began between your client's wife and his best friend resulting in the destruction of his marriage. Your initial research confirms that alienation of affection is a viable tort in North Carolina. You also identify the case of *Heller v. Somdahl*, 206 N.C. App. 313 (2010), to be relevant.

The Shepard's Report may be accessed either by navigating the tabs across the top of the document, in this case, the judicial opinion, or by clicking the button to "Shepardize document" in the Shepard's menu on the right-hand side of the page. Ten citing decisions and twenty-one other citing sources are included in the report.

Figure 18.1 Citator Example—Shepard's Using Heller v. Somdahl

Using the "Citing decisions" tab you further narrow the list of opinions to North Carolina state decisions and locate an additional decision of *Hayes v. Waltz*, 246 N.C. App. 438 (2016), as potentially helpful.

Figure 18.2 Hayes v. Waltz Case Found from Citator Report

KeyCite on Westlaw provides similar information and serves the same citator function. The KeyCite report consists of multiple tabs across the top of the document. Refer to the "Negative Treatment" and "Citing References" tabs to find primary and secondary sources that cite to *Heller v. Somdahl*. Of help in evaluating citing documents is the dept of discussion indicator. This column displays a bar chart with the green lines. The more lines, the greater the depth of discussion in the citing document. The last column in the results list identifies the headnotes associated with the citing document. Both tools, in addition to the filters on the left-hand side of the page, help to refine results and target your search.

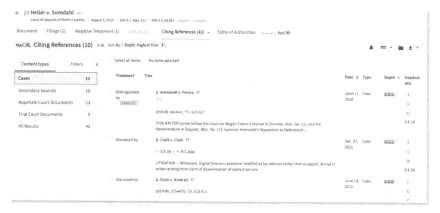

Figure 18.3 KeyCite Report

Review What You've Read

1. Name the two most popular versions of a legal citator.

2. Describe the concept of negative treatment.

3. Describe the concept of citing references.

Chapter 19

Topic and Key Number/ Researching with Digests

The Topic and Key Number system is unique to legal information published by West/Thomson Reuters, online or in print. Searching by topic and key number, or digest searching, uses the classification system developed by West Publishing over one hundred years ago and deeply rooted in the print digest. A digest is an index of published cases organized by subject matter. West initially divided the law into the over-arching topics of persons, property, contracts, torts, crimes, remedies, and government. Each of these topics is further divided into smaller, more granular, divisions and assigned a key number. New topics and key numbers continue to be added as the law evolves. There are currently over four hundred individual topics arranged in alphabetical order and over 100,000 subtopics. This classification system is flexibly conceived to cover any possible legal issue arising in a case.

A topic and key number search:

1. Locates all cases that are assigned to a given key number and thereby address the same legal issue.
2. Finds additional relevant primary and secondary sources using one topic and key number.
3. Establishes the relevance of a case for use in answering the legal question.

A complete list of topics is found at the beginning of any printed West digest volume and is available on Westlaw on the home page, under the "Get Started" tab as "Key Numbers."

Figure 19.1 Digest/Topic & Key Number in Print and on Westlaw

There are two pieces of information required to use the Topic and Key Number System: the topic and the key number. They are paired and go hand in hand. You must have both pieces of information. After identifying a relevant topic and key number in a case, a print digest, or the Topic & Key Number System on Westlaw, you may use that as a reference to locate all information assigned to the topic and key number in any West product. Cases, statutes, regulations, and secondary sources are all classified in this same system.

For example, if you are researching the issue of proximate cause in a tort matter, the broader topic is *torts*. The key number, representing a subdivision of the topic, is 119—Proximate Cause. This system of subject classification is widely effective and efficient.

Digests in Print

In print the topic and key number system is the organizational principle of the digest system. For each set of reporters there is an index known as the digest. Consider the *Southeastern Reporter*; it is a reporter that publishes cases from North Carolina, South Carolina, Virginia,

West Virginia, and Maryland in chronological order. Without an index it would be difficult to find a cases on a particular topic.

The *Southeastern Digest* is a subject matter index to the *Southeastern Reporter*. Think of the digest as the mother of all indices. The *Southeastern Digest* consists of multiple volumes arranged in alphabetical order by topic. Each headnote in each case published in the *Southeastern Reporter* is assigned to a topic and key number by West editors and the headnote, now referred to as an annotation, is arranged based on the topic and key number system within the *Southeastern Digest*. If I am interested in finding cases discussing proximate cause in tort matters, I will first find the volume or volumes covering the topic of torts and then navigate to the key number of 119 within that volume for cases specifically discussing proximate cause.

The descriptive word index, also known as the DWI, is found at the end of the digest. The DWI is a detailed subject index to the index. The DWI will refer the user to relevant topics and key numbers. In every DWI you will find a repeat of the topic and key number system and jurisdiction-specific entries representing factual situations from cases covered by the digest. The editors of the DWI use key words representing the facts and legal issues from the cases found in the associated reporter volumes to compile the index terms. If you are uncertain as to where to begin, the DWI is an excellent starting point. It helps identify the topic

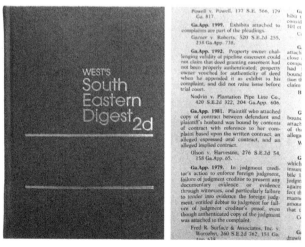

Figure 19.2 Example of South Eastern Digest 2d with Sample Page

and then the subtopic. Consider your search templates for TARP, PPT, and the W questions for entry points to the DWI.

The Digest is made current first by a pocket part and supplements and then advance sheets and mini digests in the reporter volume. At a minimum you should check the pocket part in the digest volume. If you are conducting case research using the print digests, work with your law librarian to fully update your digest search.

Finding a Topic & Key Number by a Headnote

Often the easiest way to identify a topic and key number is from the headnotes in a case already known to be relevant. This is otherwise known as the *one good case method*. The known case may come from a citator report, a cross-reference from another source, or as the result of any other search strategy employed in your research plan.

For example, you start with a known case: *Rice v. Paladin Enterprises, Inc.*, 128 F.3d 233 (4th Cir. 1997). You find that headnote 4 is directly relevant to your research. From there you note that this headnote is assigned to topic 92, Constitutional Law, further narrowed to the subtopic of XVIII, Freedom of Speech, Expression, and Press, subpart H, Law Enforcement: Criminal Conduct, and finally to the key number 1807 Particular offenses in general.

Figure 19.3 Topic & Key Number Searching on Westlaw

Finding a Topic & Key Number by Browsing

The topic and key number system is also browsable on Westlaw from the home page under the "Content types" tab, linked as "Topics & Key Numbers." On Westlaw, each topic is assigned a unique numerical representation. For example, the classification of Partnership is assigned 289. This number is not the key number but the topic. Let's say we are interested in locating cases that distinguish the partnerships entity from that of other business entities. The topic is Partnership (289), and the key number is 436. You will notice a *k* appearing in topic and key number searches. The *k* is the connector as in a terms and connector search and makes your search unique, retrieving only those documents with the desired key number. The numerical representation of the topic and key number search is 289 k 436.

Figure 19.4 Topic & Key Number Searching—Subtopic

Clicking any single topic and key number will retrieve all cases assigned to that topic and key number across all jurisdictions. In the above example, which is a result set of 150 items specifically on the topic partnerships, key number 436 Partnership distinguished from other business entities. It is not an efficient use of time to read or even skim 150 cases. Ultimately, my goal is to locate binding, primary authority, here caselaw in my jurisdiction, West Virginia. I will use the filter tools on the left side of the page to narrow my results by jurisdiction. This quickly limits my result set to two cases on the topic.

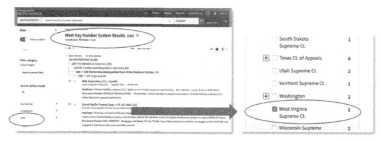

Figure 19.5 Post Search Filtering by Jurisdiction/Topic & Key Number

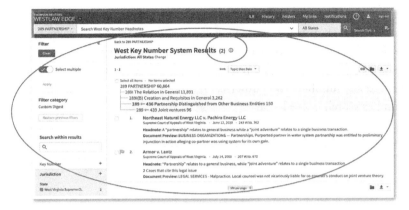

Figure 19.6 Topic & Key Number Filtered Result Set

Because of the highly classified nature of the topic and key number system, one can quickly and reliably locate highly targeted and relevant information in a minimum of time.

If you want to locate cases in North Carolina that discuss the doctrine of consideration, the researcher could find the North Carolina Digest (the jurisdictional digest), *C* for contracts, and then consideration. Under *consideration* the researcher will locate all the North Carolina cases with headnotes that discuss the doctrine of consideration. A researcher can scan the annotations included in the digest to identify cases for possible relevance. Once identified, the researcher would then locate and read the actual case for fit and relevance and possible use in an argument or memorandum of law.

Review What You've Read

1. In your own words, describe the value of the topic and key number search strategy.

2. In your own words, describe the "one good case method."

3. What two pieces of information are required for a topic and key number search?

Chapter 20

Terms and Connector Searching

How often did you use Google in the past twenty-four hours to retrieve an answer to a question? If you used Google, then you used a search engine with an algorithm and natural language searching to find an answer. In legal research we frequently use research platforms with vast amounts of information and their own algorithms to locate information. Westlaw and Lexis are the two leading subscription legal research platforms, but there are others. HeinOnline is a third favorite for law-related information. There are also free sources for legal information like Congress.gov, which we will discuss in the context of legislative history. These platforms host a multitude of databases, each containing the full text of documents. The complete text of these documents is used to retrieve results responsive to your search based on the platform's proprietary algorithm. The default on both Lexis and Westlaw is natural language searching. Natural language searching is designed to retrieve information in response to the terms input to the search box. Natural language searches rely on the proprietary (and secret) algorithm of the research platform to populate the result set. Consider the natural language search the equivalent of a self-driving car and a terms and connector search as you are driving the car. In a natural language search the algorithm does the work and gives you the information it believes to be responsive. The algorithm is proprietary so how it works is as secret as the Tesla operating system. Think about the number of instances in which a self-driving car crashed into an unexpected obstacle. It is important that you not look for just any information or answer, but rather relevant information to provide a correct answer to your client's question.

> *Remember, Westlaw and Lexis are research platforms, not sources of law themselves. As research platforms they contain hundreds of thousands of sources of law.*

Terms and connector searching, or Boolean searching, is precision-based searching. With a Boolean search you provide the instructions by defining the relationship among the search terms. You control the search. The Boolean search is powerful and searches the term or terms in exactly the manner you specify rather than the implied relationships of a natural language search, which rely on a proprietary algorithm. Think back to the list of search terms you generated in your research plan. What terms might a judge use in an opinion, in what context, and how might the terms be related? Consider the simple example of a cat bite case. If you only search for cases involving cats, you may miss the leading case as it involved a dog. What if the judge used the term *domesticated animal*? Creating a search that combines *cat*, *dog*, and *domesticated animal* is ideal. Your search might look like the following: *cat or dog or "domesticated animal"/s bite*. Translated into plain English, this search asks Westlaw or Lexis to find a document containing the word cat or dog or the exact phrase domesticated animal in the same sentence as bite.

Boolean searching is an art. It requires balancing and trial and error to refine your results to a manageable results set. You are likely to need to refine a search based on your initial result set. You want to avoid large result sets that are so broad they include a number of useless cases or junk. It is a waste of your time to sort through it all to find the few gems among the useless clutter. Skim the first ten or so results in your set for responsiveness to your search. If they are as anticipated, use your filters to further narrow your result set to a manageable number. If the results are not those anticipated, revise your search.

Tips on Boolean Searching	
Connector	*Description*
And	Narrows or restricts. The two terms connected by *and* must appear in the results.
Or	Expands the results. The appearance of only one term connected with *or* is required.
The synonym	Consider if there are multiple words a judge might use to express his holding. See the example above regarding cat, dog, domesticated animal. You need not include every synonym in the thesaurus. Balance!
Legal concepts	Boolean searching works best with terms rather than concepts, however, your goal is to find the legal concept. Think about the terms of art or legal jargon in the legal concept you seek.
Common words	Some words are too common to be meaningful in a search. If you use such a term, create context and relationship to provide meaning.

Figure 20.1 Tips on Boolean Searching

Boolean searching is premised on the use of connectors to define the relationship between terms. The connectors are the instructions; for example, a proximity connector instructs the research platform to locate one term within the defined parameter of another term. A proximity connector instructs the system to locate the term in a specific and narrow relation to the other term. Common proximity connectors are in the table below.

Common Boolean Connectors	
Connector	Description
/number	Terms must appear within the specified number of words to each other
/s	Terms must appear within the same sentence
/p	Terms must appear within the same paragraph
+s	Terms must precede the term in the same sentence

Figure 20.2 Common Boolean Connectors

AND/OR are common connectors but there are other, more nuanced, connectors that may be more helpful in creating a meaningful relationship. See the table below for additional connectors. Use the *and* connector sparingly. The proximity connectors of /s, /p, and /# are more effective. The use of quotation marks to set off a phrase is effective but can also unexpectedly limit a result set so use quotation marks judiciously. When in doubt about the order of processing, use parentheses to direct the search. Root expanders and truncation can be the searcher's best friend. Each platform/database is unique and the form and connectors will vary based on the platform/database. See the table below for additional connectors. Westlaw and Lexis offer toll-free reference attorney lines to assist the searcher. You are paying for the service so take advantage of their assistance.

Other Boolean Connectors	
Connector	Description
%/and not	And not exclude a word
!	Root expander used to include variant endings such as child, children
*	Universal character used to find terms with variable letters like drink, drank, drunk.
" "	Quotation marks around terms indicate search as a phrase
()	Parentheses instruct the search to *do this first*

Figure 20.3 Other Boolean Connectors

The steps in constructing a Boolean search are:

1. Start with the search terms you generated in your research plan. Review, revise, and select those terms to be
   included in your initial search.

2. Consider the relationship(s) you wish to define among
   the terms.

3. Draft a search statement combining search terms and
   connectors.

4. Translate your search into plain English. What instructions are you giving? What results do you expect?

5. Run your search.

6. Refine your search with the addition or deletion of terms
   or revise the connectors to expand or narrow the relationships defined between terms.

Simple principles, such as the fact that setting off an item or phrase
by parentheses in a Boolean search, can alter the order of processing
and direct the parentheses to be done first. Placing a phrase in quotation
marks can also highlight a phrase or term you intend to be searched. Understanding when *or* is processed may preclude an unintended search.
Consider the simple search of Mary Smith or Jane Jones or William
Matthews. Presumably the intended search is to locate the names of
"Mary Smith," "Jane Jones," and "William Matthews." As constructed,
the search methodology searches first for *or* thus searching for smith or
jane and jones or William first, producing a result set likely to lead to
an unintended result. An alternative might be mary /2 smith or jane /2
jones or William /2 Matthews. The simple act of writing out the search
and considering the intended result can highlight needed revisions.

In addition to the basic Boolean search, an online research platform
has other tools to enhance the research. Options to further refine your
searches in a specific database may begin by selection of a content type,
like legal periodical, or jurisdiction, like West Virginia. These initial
selections focus your research and narrow the universe of material
searched. If all I am interested in is locating a law review article with
a particular policy argument, excluding other secondary sources, then

searching exclusively for law review articles saves me time. Similarly, if I am interested in locating cases on *assumption of the risk* in West Virginia, restricting my search by jurisdiction, here West Virginia, will focus my efforts to locate primary, binding authority and save me time. I can always expand my efforts if I decide I need persuasive authority. These are pre-search filter choices that can save me time up front.

Post-search filter options provide tools for the researcher to further refine existing results. On the left side of the screen, options to refine an existing search by content type or category, like judge, date, law firm, may also prove useful. This is known as filtering or search within results.

Figure 20.4 Boolean Search with Filters (Westlaw)

Lexis and Westlaw Search Techniques: Connectors & Wildcards
1. Lexis and Westlaw automatically search for pluralized versions of words (e.g., crime—Lexis and Westlaw also look for crimes).
2. Write your search in plain language to ensure it does what you wish it to.
3. A terms and connector search is a powerful tool. Use the full range of connectors available to you. (Move beyond /s and /p).
4. Don't be afraid of trial and error. If your search result is too narrow, expand, and if they are too broad, limit.

Figure 20.5 Westlaw and Lexis Search Tips

The combination of Boolean searching with pre- and post-search filtering in research platforms like Westlaw and Lexis is a powerful tool. These are fee-based search platforms, meaning there is a cost to use the platform. That cost is often not cheap. There are excellent free sites that provide quality information that are beyond the scope of this text. Be careful to not associate free with good and paid with bad. In practice, paying the price to use a fee-based service may be less expensive than using a free service due to the increased efficiency. Educate yourself as to the benefits and detriments of the service and make an educated decision that includes cost-effectiveness. Remember anyone can and will put information on the internet. Run a Google search for the U.S. Constitution. There are some most interesting interpretations available on the Second Amendment. Publicly available information on sites like Congress.gov is readily authenticated to provide reliable information. Similarly, information on Westlaw and Lexis is authenticated and reliable. Not having to authenticate the information as good information saves time. Understanding if the information is reliable and authentic is an important check for the researcher. Finally, remember your time is valuable. Google is a powerful tool when used appropriately. However, doing research on Google to only replicate that same search on Westlaw duplicates effort and wastes billable time. Use the search strategies and tools to your benefit.

Description	Lexis +	Westlaw	Example
both terms must be present	and	& and	trademark and infringement
either term must be present	or	space between words or	car or automobile in all three systems; car automobile in Westlaw
terms must be in same sentence	/s w/s w/sent (all of these options are read as near/25)	/s w/s	design /s defect in all three systems (but Lexis + will convert this to design near/25 defect)

Table continues on next page

Table continued from last page

Description	Lexis +	Westlaw	Example
terms must be in same paragraph	/p w/p w/para (all of these options are read as near/75)	/p w/p	trademark /p infringement in all three systems (but Lexis + will convert this to trademark near/75 infringement)
terms must be within n words	/# w/# near/#	/#	breach /5 duty
terms must be within n words and in the order specified	pre/# near/#	+/n +/p +/s	john pre/3 roberts in Bloomberg and Lexis+; john +3 roberts in Bloomberg or Westlaw
exact phrase	enclose in quotes	enclose in quotes	"res judicata"
exclude a term	and not	% but not	collateral and not estoppel in Bloomberg or Lexis +; collateral % estoppel in Westlaw
grouping search terms	( )	( )	(car or automobile) /p (injury or harm)
term or phrase must appear a minimum number of times	atleast#	atleast#	atleast6 (termination)
expand root word by any number of letters	! *if used at end of search term ex child*	!	liab! would find liable or liability
permit variation for a single character	* ? replaces one letter—so use ** for two, etc.	*	wom*n would find woman or women

Description	Lexis +	Westlaw	Example
plurals	regular plurals (requiring the addition of an s) are searched automatically	plurals and possessives are searched automatically	crime would also retrieve crimes in Lexis+ and Westlaw
hyphenated terms		hyphenated form retrieves all variations of compound words	at-will searches for at will, at will, or at-will in Westlaw; must type out at-will or "at will" in Bloomberg and Lexis

Figure 20.6 Boolean Searching on Westlaw and Lexis

Review What You've Read

1. Using the terms of *dog, cat,* and *tiger,* describe the result set you anticipate retrieving using the specified connector.

   a. or

   b. and

   c. w/5

   d. but not

2. Match the following descriptive phrases with the appropriate Boolean operator.

Connector	Descriptive Phrase
And not	a. Terms with numerical proximity
Or	b. Exact phrase searching
/p	c. Include all terms
/s	d. Exclude terms
/4 (or any number)	e. Allow for variable letter(s)
Officer*	f. Terms within the same paragraph
"IIED" or any phrase/ term of art	g. Terms within the same sentence

3. Formulate a search phrase for the following fact pattern: Drew filed a false insurance claim. He claimed that his car was stolen when, in fact, it had not been. Is he liable for insurance fraud? (*Hint: Remember to use relevant alternative terms to make use of the various connectors referenced.*)

4. Evaluate the phrase "your time has value" in the context of cost-effective searching.

Chapter 21

Summary of Search Strategies

Selection of a search strategy depends upon the information you have and the type of source. Understanding when to use a specific search strategy will improve the effectiveness and efficiency of the researcher. The chart below pairs the search strategy with the source for optimal use.

Search Strategy/Source Optimal Pairings								
Search Strategy	Case	Code	Regulation	Encyclopedia	Restatement	Treatise	Periodical	A.L.R.
Find by Citation or Cross-reference	X	X	X	X	X	X	X	X
Index/TOC		X	X	X		X		
PNT		X						
Citator	X	X	X					
Topic/Key Number	X	X	X	X	X	X	X	X
Terms and Connectors	X			X	X	X	X	X

Figure 21.1 Search Strategy and Source Type

Review What You Have Read:
Search Strategies

1. What is the prerequisite for using *find by citation* or *find by cross-reference* as a search strategy?

2. What two pieces of information are required to use topic and key number as a search strategy?

3. In your own words, describe how the topic and key number search is beneficial to a researcher.

4. What types of sources are appropriate for index or table of contents searching?

5. In your own words, describe when and why to use the Popular Names Table as a search strategy.

Chapter 22

Compiling the Legislative History

Learning Objectives

1. Identify and characterize the documents, and their corresponding authority, that comprise a legislative history.

2. Employ efficient research strategies across multiple legal research platforms.

3. Identify when to incorporate legislative history into an overall research strategy.

As previously discussed in Chapter 6, a legislative history is the story of the enactment of a law based on the documents created during the process. When lawyers discuss the legislative history of an act, they refer to the process of discovering the legislative intent from the documents. To discover such intent, a researcher locates or compiles the documents created during the legislative process.

Tip

Think about each step of the legislative process and the document resulting from that step.

Steps for compiling a legislative history:

1. Ask the threshold question: does the statute contain an unresolved ambiguity? If not, the meaning of the statute is clear and there is no need to research legislative intent.

2. Determine if a court has interpreted the statutory language to resolve the ambiguity. If yes, the ambiguity is resolved, and you no longer have an ambiguity.

3. Determine if a compiled legislative history exists for this statute. If a compiled legislative history is assembled, locate that legislative history.

4. Identify descriptive information regarding the legislation. This includes the bill number, the public law number, and the Statutes at Large citation. Use the popular names table to the U.S. Code to locate the Statutes at Large citation. The Statutes at Large citation will contain the needed descriptive information.

5. Identify which research platforms, databases, or other online sources are most likely to contain the individual documents you wish to find. Note the wide variety in the different databases of a research platform. Documents and date ranges of inclusion vary greatly for legislative history materials. Confirm what is included before you begin searching. If one database or platform does not have the information, another may.

6. Conduct your research.

Compiling a legislative history is often time-consuming and frustrating. Documents may or may not be published or readily available. Because of the vast time commitment needed to compile a legislative history, the first step is to determine if someone has already done the work for you. A *compiled legislative history* is a work containing either the actual documents or citations to the documents of a legislative history for a specific piece of legislation. A compiled legislative history may appear in the form of series of citations or a multivolume work with every document. Such compiled legislative histories may be found in several places. The first place to look is your library catalog for a legislative history published in print. Westlaw contains a comprehensive collection of federal legislation. Westlaw's Arnold & Porter Legislative Histories database (named for the D.C. Law Firm by the same name) is an excellent starting point for locating a compiled legislative history for legislation enacted between 1980 and 2005.

U.S. Code Congressional and Administrative News, commonly referred to as U.S.C.C.A.N., is another source for a compiled legislative history.

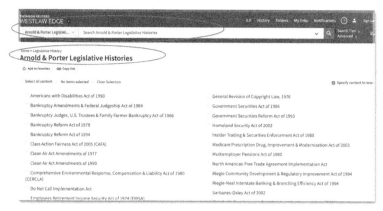

Figure 22.1 Arnold & Porter Legislative Histories (Westlaw)

U.S.C.C.A.N. is published by West and available in print and online via Westlaw. U.S.C.C.A.N. is designed to update the federal code, publishing the text of new acts during a session of Congress. U.S.C.C.A.N. has two sections, volumes with the federal session laws and a legislative history section. The U.S.C.C.A.N. legislative history is not comprehensive, but it is an excellent starting point. A U.S.C.C.A.N. legislative history will contain the key sections of the act and an edited version of the Committee Report highlighting the most important parts of the legislation. U.S.C.C.A.N. is an excellent place to start but it is important to recognize its limitations.

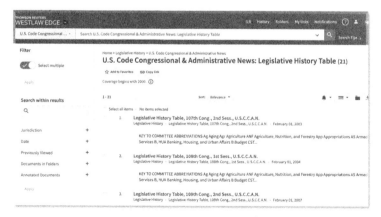

Figure 22.2 U.S.C.C.A.N. on Westlaw

The Statutes at Large are an alternative starting point for legislation passed since 1975. At the end of the text of the law is a brief summary of the legislative history of the act. The summary references citations to the committee reports of the House, Senate, and Conference, along with the dates of consideration and passage and a citation to any presidential signing statement. Citations to the *Congressional Record*, congressional hearings, and other legislative history documents are omitted.

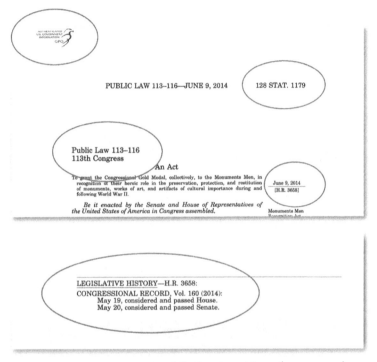

Figure 22.3 Statutes at Large and Mini Legislative History (govaccess.gov)

Platforms with compiled legislative histories include Westlaw, Legislative Insight, and HeinOnline. In addition to using the popular name of the law, the Statutes at Large citation and bill number are useful in locating a compiled legislative history. Legislative Insight and Congressional are subscription platforms from ProQuest available via many law libraries. These platforms must be used either on campus or via proxy access. Legislative Insight contains a vast collection of legislative documents and includes a number of compiled legislative histories. Congressional contains what is considered to be the most comprehensive collection of legislative history materials. In addition to containing legal periodicals, HeinOnline also contains a robust collection of legislative documents and compiled legislative histories available in the U.S. Federal Legislative History Library.

Two free research platforms are also of importance, particularly in the context of compiling a legislative history. Congress.gov at http://congress.gov and govinfo.gov at http://govinfo.gov are particularly useful. In addition to access to free and authenticated versions of the *Congressional Record* and the U.S. Code, between them a researcher will find bills, bill tracking, committee information, House and Senate calendars, and other congressional documents.

Figure 22.4 govinfo.gov and congress.gov

Authentication of electronic information is a relatively new concern associated with the explosion of sources available for free via the internet. Unfortunately, anyone can post information on the internet. Pre-internet, the publisher of materials served the function of confirming authenticity and accuracy of the information. Subscription-based online research platforms like Westlaw and Lexis continue to provide this function. The difficult task comes when the researcher is using information from the internet. Some states have adopted legislation based on the Uniform Electronic Materials Act, known as UELMA. UELMA provides the framework for the authentication, preservation, and permanent public access to legal information published in electronic format. Such provisions are intended to provide trustworthy online legal information. As of January 2022, twenty-one states had adopted UELMA laws.[1] The Government Publishing Office, better known as GPO, has addressed the issue of authenticated information directly.

> GPO has a broader responsibility not just to keep America informed, but also to take measures to provide evidence to information consumers that they can trust the information in our publication. Trust that no unauthorized changes have been made but also trust that what they are seeing is in fact the official document, has not been fabricated and has in fact been disseminated by GPO in that very form.[2]

GPO uses a digital signature on PDF documents as evidence of the integrity and authenticity of the information. This signature is evidence of the document's integrity and confirms measures were taken to prevent changes either by accident or indent to the data. The signature is also an indicium of authenticity such that a user may see visual verification of the digital document's identity, source, and ownership. The seal as indicated by the eagle logo is the signature. A user may click on the logo to verify the certification is valid and unmodified and review the signature of the digital seal.[3]

---

1. National Conference of State Legislators, Uniform Electronic Legal Material Act: State Legislation at https://www.ncsl.org/research/about-state-legislatures/uniform-electronic-legal-material-legislation.aspx (last visited April 22, 2022).

2. Govinfo.gov Authentication at https://www.govinfo.gov/about/authentication (last visited April 21, 2022).

3. *Id.*

Figure 22.5 GPO Digital Seal

Researchers using free online sources bear the additional responsibility of taking the steps to confirm that the information they are using is authentic, unaltered, and accurate.

Platforms for Compiling a Legislative History

	Bills	Comm. Reports	Compiled L. History	Floor Debates (Cong. Rec.)	Hearings	Com. Prints	Presidential Signing Statement
HeinOnline			X	X			
Congress.gov	X	X		X			
Legislative Insight (ProQuest)	X	X	X	X	X	X	X
Congressional (ProQuest)	X	X	X	X	X	X	X
Govinfo.gov	X			X			X
Westlaw	X	X	X	X	X		X
Lexis	X	X	X	X	X	X	X

Figure 22.6 Legislative History Documents and Research Platforms

If a compiled legislative history is not available, the researcher assumes the task of locating the documents. Because of the nature of a legislative history, two critical pieces of information are the starting point. The first is the bill number associated with the act and the second is the public law number. Alternative to the public law number is the citation to the Statute at Large. Keep in mind that each piece of legislation is unique and every document may not exist for every piece of legislation.

Review What You've Read

1. What are the steps for compiling a legislative history?

2. What is a compiled legislative history?

3. What is authenticated information and why is it important to use authenticated information?

Appendix

Appendix A
Authority Decision Tree

Is the source relevant to your legal question?

Yes   No   ➡   Record that you considered the source in your research log so that you do not spend time revisiting later.

Is the source primary authority or secondary authority?

Primary   Secondary   ➡   Secondary sources are always non-binding and *may be cited* depending on the type of source and its level of persuasiveness. Record the source in your research log.

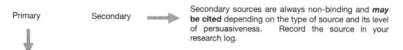

Is the primary source from a higher court in a controlling jurisdiction?

Yes   No   ➡   Primary sources from non-controlling jurisdictions are non-binding and *may* be cited as persuasive authority only. Record the source in your research log.

Primary sources **from a higher court** in the **controlling jurisdiction** are binding authority. Record the source in your research log.

Figure App A-1. Authority Decision Tree

Appendix B
Search Term Prompts

W Questions

	Unique term	Alternative and synonyms
Who		
What		
Where		
When		
Why		

People, Places, Things

	Unique term	Alternative and synonyms
People		
Places		
Things		

TARPP

	Unique term	Alternative and synonyms
Things		
Actions		
Remedies		
People		
Places		

Appendix C
The Research Plan Template

Legal Research Plan

Step 1: Identify the legal issue or issues and prepare a preliminary issue statement for each.

    A. Identify the controlling jurisdiction:

    B. Identify the legal question to research:

    C. List the determinative facts:

    D. Combine parts A, B, and C above to draft a preliminary issue statement:

Under *[applicable law]*, does *[legal question]*, when *[determinative facts]*.

Step 2: Generate search terms.

You are required to complete only one of the following based on the instructions for each research exercise.

W Questions

	Unique term	Alternative and synonyms
Who		
What		
Where		
When		
Why		

Step 2 continues on next page

Step 2 continued from last page

People, Places, Things

	Unique term	Alternative and synonyms
People		
Places		
Things		

TARPP

	Unique term	Alternative and synonyms
Things		
Actions		
Remedies		
People		
Places		

Step 3: Drafting terms and connectors search statements.

Use the search terms above to draft at least three (3) unique search statements incorporating terms and connectors that you may use in an online research platform.

	Statement	Translate your search statement into plain language
Statement #1		
Statement #2		
Statement #3		

Step 4: Generate a potential list of sources and their order of use (and print or online).

This a brainstorming step. What types of sources will contain legal information to help answer your legal question? In which primary sources will you find the law? In which secondary sources will you find information interpreting the law? This step must be done before *you begin your research.*

Order	Source	Why will you use this source?
1		
2		
3		
4		

Steps 1 through 4 constitute a completed legal research plan. Execute your research plan and document your research in the research log.

Appendix D
Instructions for Completing
a Research Plan

Step 1: Identify the legal issue or issues and prepare a preliminary issue statement for each.

A. Identify the controlling jurisdiction: ◄┄┄

> Jurisdiction refers to binding authority and is not the same as venue, which refers to the court where a case may be tried.
> Example:
> Jurisdiction = West Virginia; Venue = Monongalia County District Court. Record only jurisdiction in this part of the research plan.

> The legal question is the foundation of a legal research project. Briefly and in your own words, what unresolved legal question is presented by the facts?

B. Identify the legal question to research:

C. List the determinative facts: ◄┄┄┄

> Determinative facts are facts on which the legal question will turn. If the determinative fact changes, then the outcome of the case would also change. In your research plan record only the determinative facts. (Isolate individual facts. Do not copy/paste from the hypo).

D. Combine parts A, B, and C above to draft a preliminary issue statement:

Under *[applicable law]*, does *[legal question]*, when *[determinative facts]*.

> An issue statement is composed of three parts: the applicable law, the legal question, and the determinative facts. See CHRISTINE COUGHLIN ET AL., A LAWYER WRITES A PRACTICAL GUIDE TO LEGAL ANALYSIS 219 (2d ed. 2013).

Step 2: Generate search terms.

Search terms are the building blocks of a terms and connectors search statement. As part of a research plan, it is important to identify terms that you would include in a terms and connectors search statement or would use to navigate a table of contents or index.

There are multiple methods to help generate search terms that describe a factual situation and legal question. Below are options including the "W questions," "People, Places, Things"; and "TARPP," or "Things, Actions, Remedies, People, Place." Because courts and legislators vary their language to describe similar things, it is important to identify alternative terms and synonyms to capture all relevant legal information on a single issue.

Templates for each of these methods are in this worksheet. You are required to complete only one of the following based on the instructions for each research exercise.

In this example, "who" uses two unique terms and their corresponding alternatives and synonyms.

Example: W Questions

	Unique term	Alternative and synonyms
Who	Instructor Student	teacher, professor ◀············· pupil, classmate
What	Education	Instruction, lesson, degree, diploma, scholarship, learning
Where	Campus	School, university, classroom, "lecture hall"
When	Semester	"school day," "academic year," "class period"
Why	IEP	"individualized education plan," accommodation ▶

This is an example of a *phrase*. Phrases in quotes will be retrieved exactly as written in a terms and connectors search statement. If you wish to use a phrase to describe the factual situation, record it here with quotes. If you do not intend to use the phrase in a T&C search, break down the phrase into individual search terms.

Step 2 continues on next page

Step 2 continued from last page

W Questions

	Unique term	Alternative and synonyms
Who		
What		
Where		
When		
Why		

People, Places, Things

	Unique term	Alternative and synonyms
People		
Places		
Things		

TARPP

	Unique term	Alternative and synonyms
Things		
Actions		
Remedies		
People		
Places		

Step 3: Drafting terms and connectors search statements.

Use the search terms above to draft at least three (3) unique search statements incorporating terms and connectors that you may use in an online research platform.

	Statement	Translate your search statement into plain language
Statement #1	(Instructor OR teacher OR professor) /s (student OR pupil) AND (IEP OR "individualized educational plan")	At least one of the terms: instructor, teacher, or professor in the same sentence as either student or pupil in the same document as either IEP or the phrase "individualized educational plan"
Statement #2		
Statement #3		

Terms and connectors search statements instruct an online research platform like Westlaw Edge or Lexis+ how to relate search terms to one another. By using terms and connectors search statements, you control your search results precisely rather than relying on the search platform's algorithms. Refer to Chapter 20 in the textbook for a more detailed discussion of terms and connectors searching.

Step 4: Generate a potential list of sources and their order of use (and print or online).

Order	Source	Why will you use this source?
1	American Jurisprudence 2d	A national encyclopedia like Am. Jur. will offer a broad overview of legal concepts related to education and IEPs.
2	United States Code Annotated	The U.S.C.A. contains the controlling federal statute regarding IEPs. This is the annotated version of the code that will also refer me to other related primary sources and secondary sources.
3		
4		

Terms and connectors search statements instruct an online research platform like Westlaw or Lexis+ how to relate search terms to one another. By using terms and connectors search statements, you control your search results precisely rather than relying on the search platform's algorithms. Refer to Chapter 20 in the textbook for a more detailed discussion of terms and connectors searching.

Steps 1 through 4 constitute a completed legal research plan. Execute your research plan and document your research in the research log.

Appendix E
The Research Log Template

A research log documents the sources found while executing your research plan. Your log will include sources of varying degrees of relevance and utility. It is a record of your work. Each log entry describes the source and evaluates it on a number of important criteria. Use the blank template of the research log to complete research exercises along with the "Instructions for Completing a Research Log" provided.

Source 1:	Source citation:	
	Authority:	Type of authority:
		Weight of authority:
	Description of search:	Search strategy:
		Description of steps taken:
	Currency:	
	Validity:	
	Analyze the authority: (Choose the relevant prompts from the instructions to answer thoroughly)	

Appendix F
Instructions for Completing
a Research Log

A research log documents the sources found while executing your research plan. Your log will include sources of varying degrees of relevance and utility. It is a record of your work. Each log entry describes the source and evaluates it on a number of important criteria as described below. Use the blank template of the research log to complete research exercises.

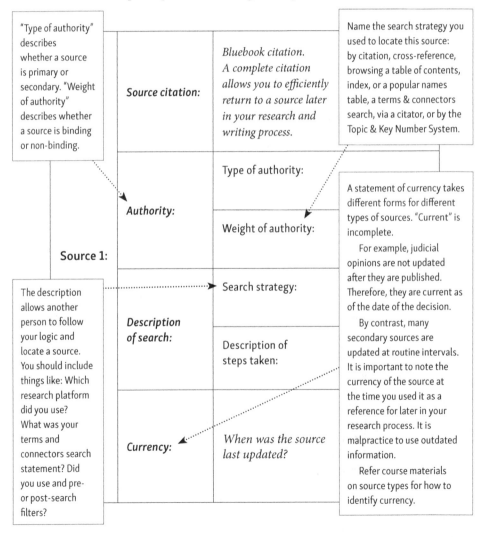

"Type of authority" describes whether a source is primary or secondary. "Weight of authority" describes whether a source is binding or non-binding.

Source citation:

Bluebook citation. A complete citation allows you to efficiently return to a source later in your research and writing process.

Name the search strategy you used to locate this source: by citation, cross-reference, browsing a table of contents, index, or a popular names table, a terms & connectors search, via a citator, or by the Topic & Key Number System.

Source 1:

Authority:

Type of authority:

Weight of authority:

A statement of currency takes different forms for different types of sources. "Current" is incomplete.

For example, judicial opinions are not updated after they are published. Therefore, they are current as of the date of the decision.

By contrast, many secondary sources are updated at routine intervals. It is important to note the currency of the source at the time you used it as a reference for later in your research process. It is malpractice to use outdated information.

Refer course materials on source types for how to identify currency.

The description allows another person to follow your logic and locate a source. You should include things like: Which research platform did you use? What was your terms and connectors search statement? Did you use and pre- or post-search filters?

Description of search:

Search strategy:

Description of steps taken:

Currency:

When was the source last updated?

Source 1:	Validity:	Is the source "good law"? What citator did you use? Applies to primary authorities only.	Shepard's and KeyCite are the two major citators that you will use to determine validity. A complete answer will describe the subsequent treatment of a primary source and indicate whether there is negative treatment that overturns, overrules, or questions the underlying law. Absence of negative treatment indicates "good law." For example, "According to KeyCite, there is no negative subsequent treatment of this case. Therefore, it remains good law."
	Analyze the authority: (Choose the relevant prompts from the instructions to answer thoroughly)	Use as many of the following prompts as necessary and as applicable to analyze the authority based on the type of source: • Does it explain a legal concept? • Does it help to identify new legal vocabulary? • Is it factually analogous? • Is it the leading case or controlling statute? • Is it a primary source that provides a rule of law? If yes, what is the rule? Apply the rule to the facts and explain. • Does it expand upon or revise a previous rule? • Does it help to identify other relevant primary or secondary sources. i.e., cross-references? • Will you use this in a final work product? If yes, how?	

This is a legal analysis of the authority. How will you use the authority to solve the legal problem?

Appendix G
Exemplar from govinfo.gov—Statutes at Large

PUBLIC LAW 113–116—JUNE 9, 2014   128 STAT. 1179

Public Law 113–116
113th Congress

An Act

To grant the Congressional Gold Medal, collectively, to the Monuments Men, in recognition of their heroic role in the preservation, protection, and restitution of monuments, works of art, and artifacts of cultural importance during and following World War II.

June 9, 2014
[H.R. 3658]

Be it enacted by the Senate and House of Representatives of the United States of America in Congress assembled,

Monuments Men Recognition Act of 2014.
31 USC 5111 note.

SECTION 1. SHORT TITLE.

This Act may be cited as the "Monuments Men Recognition Act of 2014".

SEC. 2. FINDINGS.

The Congress finds the following:

(1) On June 23, 1943, President Franklin D. Roosevelt formed the "American Commission for the Protection and Salvage of Artistic and Historic Monuments in War Areas".

(2) The Commission established the Monuments, Fine Arts, and Archives ("MFAA") Section under the Allied Armies.

(3) The men and women serving in the MFAA Section were referred to as the "Monuments Men".

(4) These individuals had expertise as museum directors, curators, art historians, artists, architects, and educators.

(5) In December 1943, General Dwight D. Eisenhower empowered the Monuments Men by issuing orders to all commanders that stated they must respect monuments "so far as war allows".

(6) Initially the Monuments Men were intended to protect and temporarily repair the monuments, churches, and cathedrals of Europe suffering damage due to combat.

(7) Hitler and the Nazis engaged in a pre-meditated, mass theft of art and stored priceless works in thousands of art repositories throughout Europe.

(8) The Monuments Men adapted their mission to identify, preserve, catalogue, and repatriate almost 5,000,000 artistic and cultural items which they discovered.

(9) This magnitude of cultural preservation was unprecedented during a time of conflict.

(10) The Monuments Men grew to no more than 350 individuals and joined front line military forces; two Monuments Men lost their lives in action.

(11) Following the Allied victory, the Monuments Men remained abroad to rebuild cultural life in Europe through organizing art exhibitions and concerts.

Figure App G-1. Public Law 113-116

Appendix H
Glossary of Common Research Terms

Administrative order or decision	an administrative act or document expressing the outcome or decision of an agency made in accordance with established procedures.
Advance Sheet	a pamphlet with the most recently published opinions of a court or group of courts with the pagination and volume number of the reporter volume in which the opinion will ultimately appear.
Agency	a part of the executive branch created by a delegation of authority by legislative act with the authority to issue rules and/or adjudicate disputes subject to the scope of authority delegated by the legislature.
Annotation	(1) a brief summary of the law and facts of a case interpreting a statute included in an annotated code; or (2) an explanatory essay on a significant point of law.
Authority	that which binds or influences a court.
Bill	the document that contains a draft of proposed legislation.
Black Letter Law	a generally accepted legal rule.
Caselaw	the law appearing in a judicial opinion.
Casebook	the textbook used in law courses containing a collection of highly edited appellate opinions.
Citation	a reference to an authority cited in support of an argument.
Citator	an online tool that validates the status of primary authority as continuing to be good law; may also serve as a research tool to identify subsequent judicial opinions in the history of the case or cases that interpret the case. May also be in multivolume book form. Shepard's Citations and KeyCite are the most frequently used.

Civil law	Roman Law codified in the Justinian Code predominantly found in continental Western Europe and Louisiana. Key characteristic is the significant reliance on the code rather than the judicial opinion.
Code	Subject matter arrangement in a prearranged classified order of the statutes with general applicability and force of law. Codification refers to the process of the collection and subject matter arrangement of law into the Code.
Common law	Law created by judicial opinion documenting the custom discovered by a court. The basis of the Anglo-American legal system derived from England.
Constitution	a system of fundamental principles that creates the framework of a political unit. May be written or unwritten.
Digest	an index to published or reported cases with annotations or brief summaries of the holding of the court on a point of law arranged by subject matter, court, and jurisdiction.
Docket number	the filing number sequentially assigned to a matter by the clerk of court at the initiation of the lawsuit.
En Banc	an instance of oral argument in which the entire bench of a court participates in the hearing and ultimate decision.
Encyclopedia	a work with essays on statements of an area of law, arranged by topic, containing footnote references to cases on point.
Executive order	a declaration by an executive with the force of law based on existing statutory power.
Headnote	a brief summary of a legal rule, point of law, or significant facts in an opinion prepared by an editor, preceding the opinion and used to briefly scan the case for relevance.
Holding	the rule of law issued by the court as applied to the facts of the case for resolution of the matter.

Hornbook	the name given the student treatise in an area of law summarizing the law in essay format.
Jurisdiction	the power granted by legislative or constitutional act to render legally binding decisions over persons or property in a specific geographic area in which area the decisions of the court or legislative acts are considered binding authority.
Key number	the permanent number assigned by an editor of West to a specific point of law.
Law Review also Law Journal	a legal periodical, usually student edited.
Legislative History	information found in the documents of the legislative process that provides information regarding the intent of the legislative body as a whole of the underlying statute.
Legislative Intent	intent of the legislative body as a whole.
Mandatory authority	authority that a given court is required to follow.
National Reporter System	the reporters published by West intended to publish and index all cases designated with precedential value from all state and federal courts.
Dictum (also obiter dictum)	incidental comment not necessary to the decision.
Opinion	Expression of the reasons for the outcome of a case. *Majority opinion*—an opinion that represents the principle of law a majority of the judges considered operative in a given decision; considered to have the most precedential value. *Concurring opinion*—one written by a judge that agrees with the outcome of the matter as stated in the majority opinion but for different reasons. *Dissenting opinion*—one written by a judge that disagrees with the outcome and reasoning stated in the majority opinion. *Plurality opinion*—a decision in which less than a majority agree as to the reasoning, but a majority agree to the outcome.

Opinion, cont.	*Per curiam*—an opinion by a court stating a decision with no author designated. *Memorandum opinion*—a concise statement of the holding of the case.
Persuasive authority	reasoning that a court may but is not required to follow.
Pocket part	a supplement in paper form inserted into the back cover of a book.
Popular Names Table	a table listing cases or statutes by their common or popular name with an associated citation.
Proclamation	the formal statement declaring to the public that the government has acted in a specific manner.
Public Law	an act with general application to all persons in such jurisdiction.
Regional Reporter	a subdivision of the National Reporter System that includes state court decisions from a defined geographical area.
Regulations	also known as *rules*; orders issued by a governmental agency to carry out the intent of the law.
Reporter	a series of print volumes with a collection of published judicial decisions arranged by jurisdiction, court, or subject.
Restatements of the Law	systematic restatement of the common law published by the American Law Institute.
Session law	laws enacted by a legislature published in chronological order at the conclusion of a legislative session.
Shepardize	to confirm the validity of a primary authority using Shepard's Citator.
Slip law	the initial instance of the published act in pamphlet form.
Slip Opinion	The initial instance of the publication of a judicial opinion issued at the time of the decision.

Stare Decisis	the doctrine that requires a court to follow an established principle of law applicable to a set of facts when the legal issue and factual predicate are substantially the same.
Statutes	the acts of a legislature.
Statutes at Large	the official compilation of the acts of the United States Congress arranged in chronological order by Public Law number. The official law for all titles of the U.S. Code not enacted into positive law.
Style or Caption of a Case	A statement of the parties to a lawsuit as indicated in the heading of a case.
Treatise	A work online or in a single volume or multivolume set containing a critical, explanatory, interpretive, or informational discussion of an area of law with substantial citations to primary authority. A book.
Unofficial reporter or code	court reports or a code published in the absence of legislative or judicial authority.

Index